INFORMATION REVOLUTION

Lynn Myring and Ian Graham

Designed by **Roger Boffey and Iain Ashman**
Consultant editor: **Robin Mudge**

**Illustrated by Simon Roulstone, Chris Lyon,
Martin Newton, Jeremy Gower, Mick Gillah, Janos Marffy,
Mike Saunders, Roger Boffey**

Contents

- 3 **About the information revolution**
- 4 **The cabled city**
- 6 **The new technology**
- 8 **How computers handle information**
- 10 **Computer shopping**
- 12 **Electronic banking**
- 14 **TV technology**
- 16 **Information on your TV screen**
  - 18 **Viewdata**
  - 22 **Teletext**
  - 24 **Telesoftware**
- 26 **The electronic office**
- 28 **Word processing**
- 30 **Future phones**
- 32 **What does "telecommunications" mean?**
- 34 **Satellite communications**
- 36 **Fibre optics**
- 38 **The revolution in factories**
- 40 **Video technology**
- 42 **Microchips**
- 44 **Communicating with computers**
- 46 **Information revolution words**
- 48 **Index**

First published in 1983
by Usborne Publishing Ltd, 20 Garrick Street, London WC2 9BJ

Copyright © 1983 Usborne Publishing Ltd

All rights reserved. No part of this publication may be reproduced, stored in any form or by any means mechanical, electronic, photocopying, recording, or otherwise without the prior permission of the publisher.

About the information revolution

Many of the things you do depend upon you receiving and acting on information from other people. Catching a train, making a phone call, watching TV, buying a hamburger and going to the cinema all involve information being stored, processed and communicated. At the moment most information is stored on paper – as books, magazines, newspapers, timetables and so on. You may not be aware of it but methods of dealing with information are being revolutionized by microelectronics and computers. Computers can store vast amounts of information, not just words but pictures and sounds too. They can also process it millions of times faster than people can. You probably use computers every day without even realising it. In the supermarket your bill may be added up and printed out by a

computer terminal disguised as an ordinary cash register. The money you use to pay for the shopping may have come out of a different computer terminal at a bank. Even your voice can be electronically processed so that it travels as tiny flashes of laser light through a fibre optic telephone network, without you noticing any difference in your phone calls. Many of these things, which you will find out more about in this book, are known as information technology, or IT for short.

Information technology is not always obvious from the surface. Recent developments in microelectronics have made it possible to fit tiny "computers on a

chip" and memory chips inside everyday machines such as cars, TVs, phones and even washing machines. These are programmed to make such familiar objects

more efficient and versatile, able to process the information you put in and act on it. The supermarket cash register, for example, may be recording how much of what has been sold and working out what to order, as well as dealing with your bill.

Processing information is important but it is only part of the story. Communication is an equally vital part of the information revolution. The phone, radio and TV have all revolutionized communications between people. Information technology is providing communication between machines and people and also directly between machines. The supermarket cash register may be communicating over the phone line with another computer at a

warehouse and ordering stock that the shop needs. With IT, you too can communicate with distant computers. You can use them to shop, bank and work from home, search electronic libraries and information services on computer, get programs for your home computer and play electronic games with other people over the phone. In fact all these things are possible now and already available in some places. They will become more widespread as the information revolution advances.

The cabled city

Information technology is gradually bringing changes to all areas of life – home, work, entertainment, even everyday chores like shopping. It is providing extra ways of doing things, rather than just replacing old ones. People still write letters and read newspapers today, although the phone and TV exist. The information revolution gives another alternative; that of sending electronically prepared text and pictures by cables, like phone lines.

Most of these information technology alternatives depend upon good, two-way telecommunications links, able to carry computer data, TV channels, graphics, phone calls, text, video pictures and any other information that people want to transmit. Some links are already provided by ordinary phone and cable TV networks. As the information revolution spreads, better telecommunication networks that are specially designed for communications between the new technology machines will be set up. These will use the latest developments, such as fibre optics, lasers, microelectronics and computer control to bring about the "cabled city" of the future and the things it offers, described here.

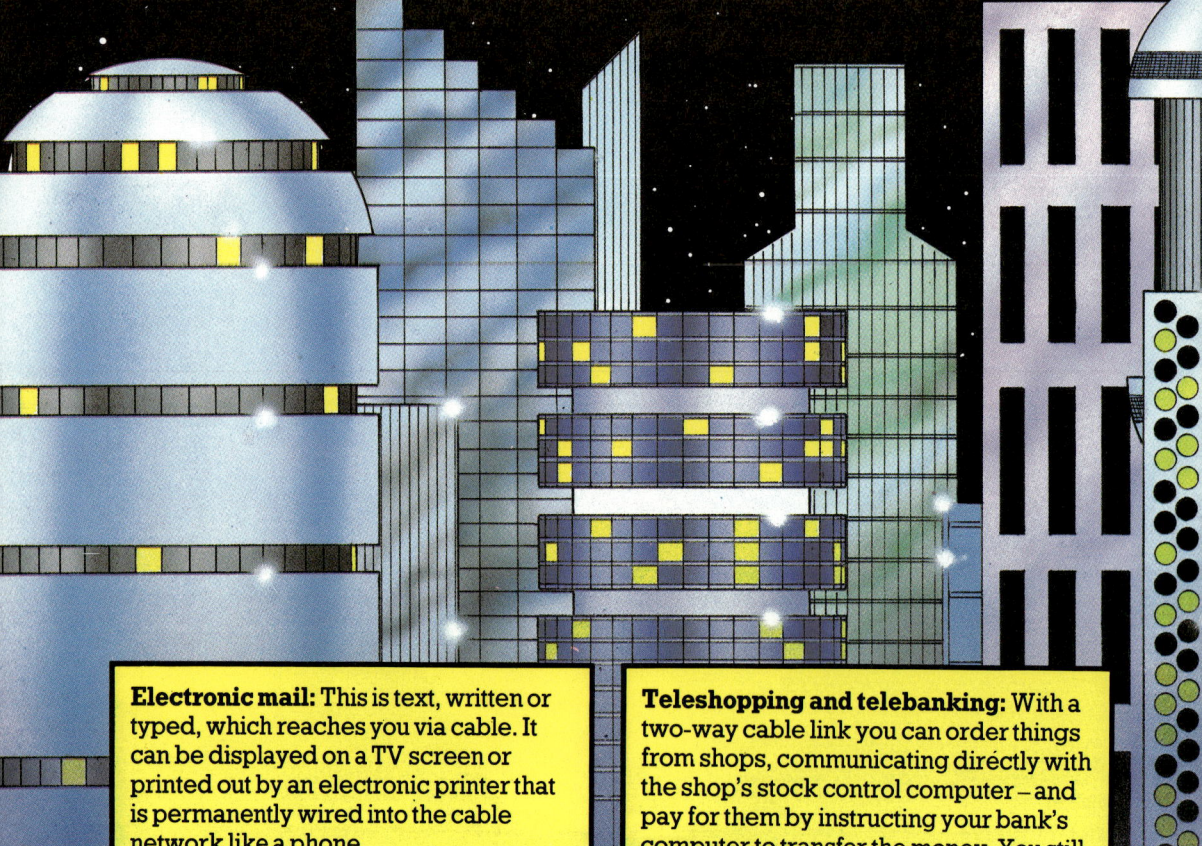

Electronic mail: This is text, written or typed, which reaches you via cable. It can be displayed on a TV screen or printed out by an electronic printer that is permanently wired into the cable network like a phone.

Electronic publishing: Newspapers, magazines, books, in fact any kind of printed material can reach you by cable. You could call up whatever you wanted, look at it on a TV and get copies made by your colour facsimile machine of the parts you want to keep.

Teleshopping and telebanking: With a two-way cable link you can order things from shops, communicating directly with the shop's stock control computer – and pay for them by instructing your bank's computer to transfer the money. You still have to wait for delivery though.

Videotex: This is a computerized information service which reaches you by phone or TV. You can use it to look up pages of useful information. Libraries of electronic information are known as databases and getting information out of them is called accessing.

Home: The information revolution will bring more electronic equipment into use at home. The whole lot could be under the control of a central home computer that you could reach over the phone when you are out. You could instruct it to turn on lights and heating, record a TV programme onto video tape, heat your dinner, take and send phone messages, get a print of an electronic newspaper and so on.

Work: With good telecommunications an office, factory or school does not have to be in one place. Computers and the people using them can communicate as easily over long distances as in one large building. In the cabled city, teachers can mark their pupils' work, engineers can control robots in automated factories, doctors can question patients, travel agents can book holidays, bankers can monitor customers' overdrafts, and so on, all working from home and using databases of information that needs to be shared.

Entertainment: The information revolution will bring more TV channels, not only broadcast as they are now but also by satellite and cable. There will be specialist channels concentrating on different areas and even more material recorded on video tapes and discs. Computer software will also reach you by cable and there could be mass games played by thousands of people over the phone. New technology is improving ways of recording and playing music. Many films, like *Tron*, could not have been made without computers.

The new technology

The information revolution is bringing new machines into common use and changing the ways that familiar ones work and how you use them. Only a few years ago pocket calculators were expensive and much larger than they are now. Today they are small, slim, cheap and can do much more than just arithmetic – some tell the time, play tunes, work out biorhythms, tell fortunes and can be programmed. Cassette recorders have been given a new use as data storage systems for home computers – themselves almost unheard of a few years ago. These changes are being brought about by microelectronics, especially the silicon chip*, which makes machines more efficient, reliable and able to do more things.

New technology at work

This picture shows some of the new technology at work. The TV is showing a weather map of Europe made up from information from a weather satellite and sent out by videotex. The printer is wired into the phone network and is receiving electronic mail typed on a home computer keyboard, like the one shown here. With the addition of a device called a modem (see page 19) any computer can be turned into a communications terminal. The cassette machine is used for storing computer data and can contain a program to control the micro-robot. The video disc player has an interactive disc all about bicycle maintenance on the turntable and the telephone is programmed to pass any in-coming calls to another number.

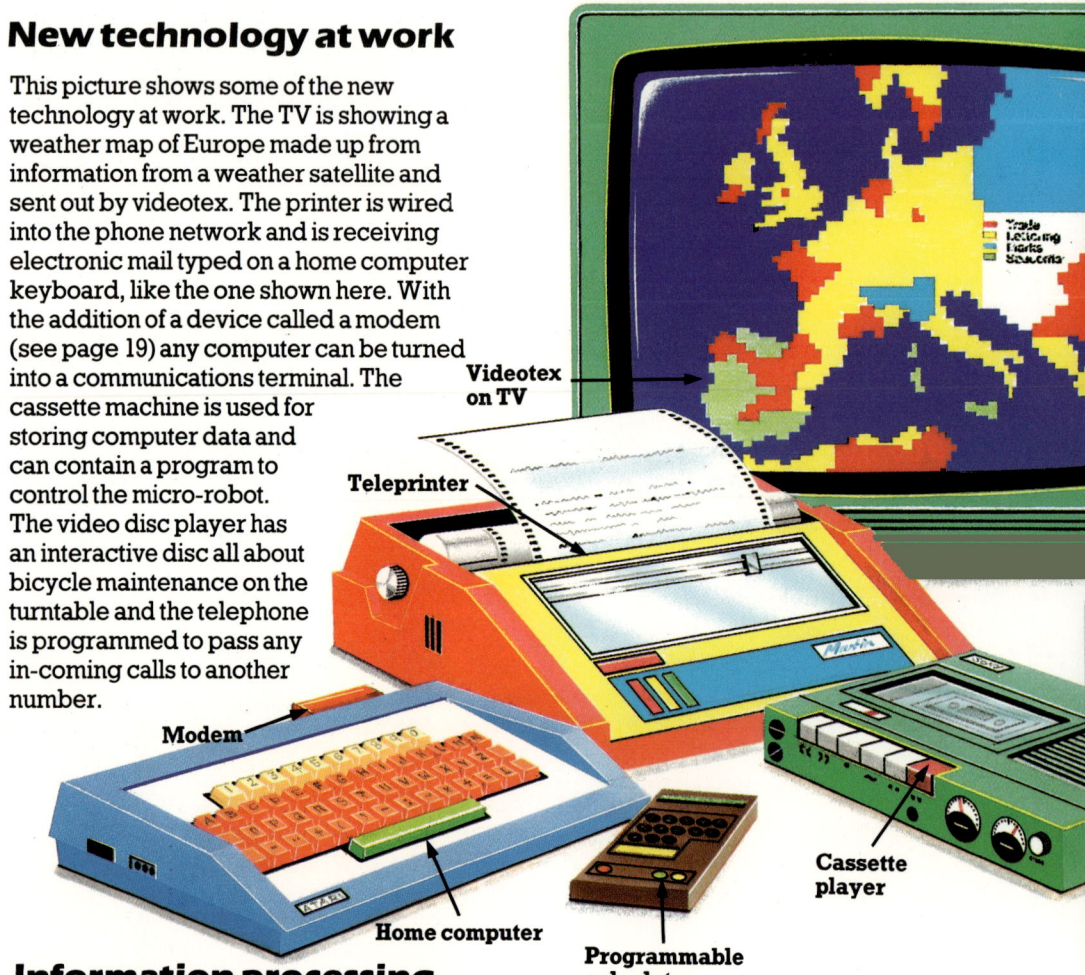

Videotex on TV

Teleprinter

Modem

Home computer

Programmable calculator

Cassette player

Information processing

Most information reaches you as words and pictures simply because this is the best way for you to understand it. Microelectronic machines deal with information in the form of electrical pulses. Any sort of information – written and spoken words, pictures, measurements, sounds, even smells – can be turned into electrical pulses and "understood" by a microchip. Information is already often stored and transmitted electronically. It then has to be processed by a machine into a form that people can understand; TV broadcasts or cassette tapes for example.

Computers are particularly good at processing information and do it so fast that they have given us new ways of looking at it. The way that computers store and retrieve information is revolutionary too. A computer can look up the electronic

*See page 42 for more about chips.

This micro-robot arm can move in response to commands typed on a computer keyboard.

Video disc player

Telephone

Driving with new technology

Driving a car is a complex task which involves processing a lot of information from many sources – what is the best route to take, how to run the engine efficiently, should you turn the wipers and lights on, what speed can you go and so on. New technology can help with all these and more. To find the best route you could load a video map of the area, key in the place you want to go, tune the radio to pick up data on traffic conditions and then follow the arrows displayed on the screen by the dashboard computer, which is programmed to use all this information. It will also automatically control the motor, lights, wipers, speed, heaters and even things impossible to change now, like the suspension and aerodynamics. Speech synthesizer chips will remind you to fasten your seat belt or drive slower and even tell you when there is a fault and how to mend it. All of these features have been tested experimentally and some are even available now.

Intelligent machines

Machines that are controlled by microchips are sometimes referred to as "smart" or "intelligent". This is because they seem to be responding to information in a clever way; doing different things in different situations. In fact, they are just following a set of instructions, called a program, electronically stored in a memory chip. The program says "If this happens... do that." A camera, for example, may contain a program that tells it how to work out the correct exposure for the light level and film speed. It automatically responds to information coming from the light meter by adjusting the length of time that the shutter stays open. New technology machines are often much easier to use than the non-microchip kind.

equivalent of a whole library of books in a split second. This processing speed and fast access to information means that computers can calculate things that would be impossible for people to work out because it would take too long. Space travel, for example, would be impossible without computers. Even everyday things like driving a car can be greatly improved by microelectronics, as explained above.

How computers handle information

Computers work using a very simple code made up of pulses of electricity. There are just two signals in this code – on and off – which are written down as 1s and 0s. This computer code is called a binary digital code; binary because it uses two signals and digital because it is a kind of number system.

When processed by computer all information, whatever its form, is converted into binary digital code. Pictures, text, sounds, measurements, in fact everything is turned into a stream of 1s and 0s. Information in this computerized state is known as digital information. (The word "information" is often replaced with data.) Non-digital information is called analogue. You can see the difference between analogue and digital information by comparing an ordinary watch with a digital one. The ordinary watch shows the time by constantly and smoothly moving the hands round the dial – an analogue measurement. The digital watch shows the time in numbers that change in steps, say once every second.

Bits and bytes

This telecommunications satellite is sending digital phone calls and computer data from one side of Earth to the other.

Each on and off pulse of computer code is known as a bit, short for binary digit. Most computers and other microelectronic machines use groups of eight bits to represent pieces of information, such as a letter of the alphabet, number and so on. A group of eight bits is called a byte.

Inside the computer the bits are represented by electricity, a high voltage for a 1 and a low voltage for a 0. Any sort of information can be converted into bytes if it is first turned into a stream of electricity. Lots of information reaches you as analogue electricity already – your voice is turned into electricity by a phone, music is turned into electricity when recorded and TVs make pictures from electricity. The advantage of having information as a digital code rather than a stream of analogue electricity is that it can then be directly processed by computer. This is the key to the information revolution.

What does digital information look like?

Digital information does not have to be a code of pulses of electricity. Just as it can be written down as 1s and 0s, it can also be represented in other ways. These pictures show some of them. The satellite above is beaming digital information through space.

▲ The digital code can be pulses of light. This picture shows a fibre optic cable which transmits digital data as flashes of laser light.

Solar panels provide the satellite with electricity.

Dish aerials receive, boost and transmit the signals.

Signals going to dish aerial

The digital signals are sent as two radio frequencies.

Processing digital information

Digital data has several advantages over ordinary information. Text stored electronically on floppy disk, for example, takes up much less room than the paper necessary for the same information. The main advantage, though, is that digital data can be handled by computers and other microprocessor-based new technology. Electronically stored information can be called up and easily changed using a computer. It can also be sent over the phone to another computerized machine, such as a printer.

Existing technologies are adopting digital techniques too. Digitally recorded music sounds better than ordinary recordings as it can cope better with the highest and lowest notes. Digital compact audio discs never wear out either, as they are played by a laser beam that does not touch the surface.

▼ The first computers were given digital information coded on strips of paper or cards. The 1s are represented by the holes, the 0s by the no-holes.

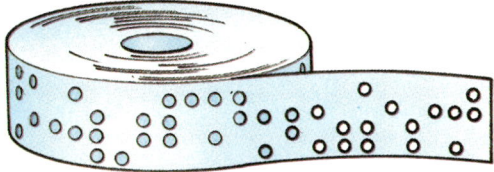

▼ Compact audio discs use a similar system for recording sounds. There are microscopic pits and no-pits in the reflective surface of the discs, which are read by a laser beam.

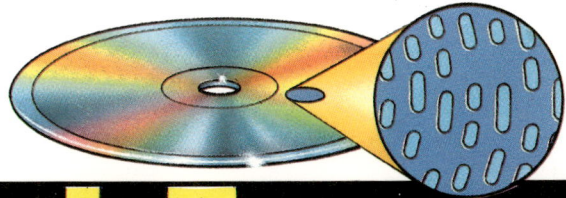

▲ Bar codes use black and white stripes to reflect a digital code of light/no light. This can be used to represent any kind of information, from music to computer programs.

▲ Digital information can be transmitted as two tones of sound – high and low. These can travel over the phone like any other kinds of sound.

9

Computer shopping

Computers already play an important part in shopping. Big shops, especially chain stores with branches all over the country, have to deal with very large amounts of information. They have to keep enough goods on the shelves for customers to buy, re-order stock that is low, decide which things are selling well, make sure that the price is right and so on. Computers are particularly good at monitoring this sort of flow of information. An automated system like the one shown here can keep up to date on sales and stock figures, help work out prices and even be programmed to re-order goods itself.

Stock control

When goods are delivered to the shop this information is put into the shop's computer. It then knows how much of what is in stock. As goods are sold the cash register terminals pass on this data to the computer. The computer is programmed to compare these two

This picture shows some shopping being checked out at a supermarket till. The cash register is not only a till for holding money but also a computer terminal, linked to other terminals in the shop and the main stock control computers at head office.

Bar codes

Lots of goods in the shops are now printed with a pattern of black and white stripes called a bar code. Bar codes are a way of storing digital information that can be fed straight into a computer. The black and white lines represent 1s and 0s and can be read by light. When a beam of light is passed over the bar code only the white stripes reflect back any light. This is picked up by a photodetector, which produces a pulse of electricity when it receives light. So the black and white bar code is translated into on/off pulses of electricity. The information encoded as a bar code is actually a 13 digit number. Each product has its own, unique number which tells the computer all about it.

Blogg's beans bar code

This picture shows the imaginary bar code for a tin of Blogg's baked beans. Part of the bar code tells the computer that it is a Blogg's product and all Blogg's goods will have these digits. Other digits pass on the information that it is baked beans – all makes of baked beans will include these. The rest of the digits give information about the size of the tin. The price is not included as part of the bar code as this may change. The check-out terminal looks up the prices, which are stored in its memory.

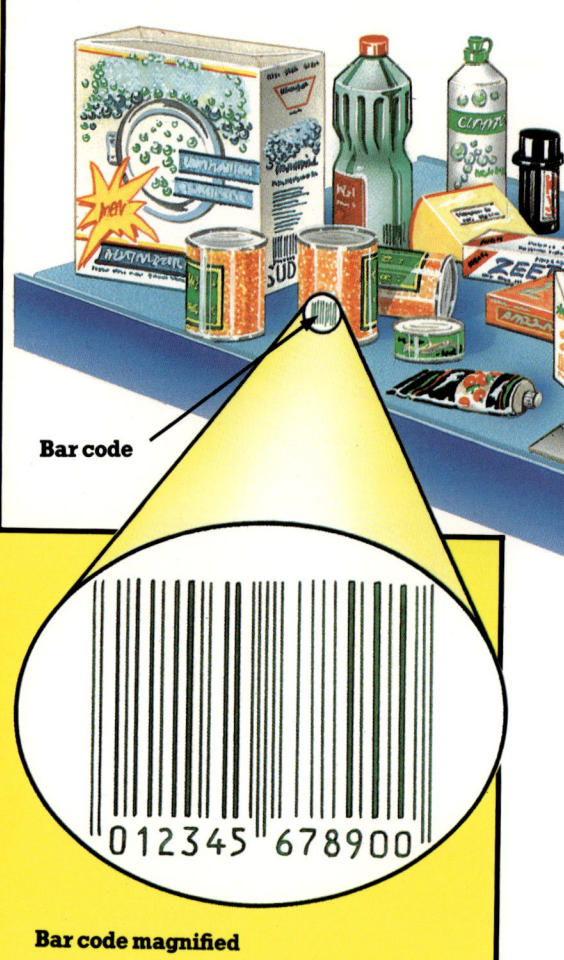

Bar code

Bar code magnified

figures and work out how quickly things are selling. It can then tell when to re-order different products. Stock ordering can be automated too, by programming the computer to print out the orders or even to communicate directly with manufacturers' computers over the telephone.

The cash register

This cash register has a memory containing the bar code numbers and prices of all the goods in the shop. When it gets a reading from the laser scanner it looks up the number and displays the product name and price on its display screens and prints it out as a receipt too. The cash register also records what has been sold on a tiny built-in cassette recorder. This information is used for stock control.

Usually it is necessary for only one of the cash registers to be an "intelligent" terminal with a memory. All the other cash registers are connected to it and make use of its memory to look up products and store sales information. In some systems all the cash registers are "dumb" and get their information from a computer somewhere else in the shop.

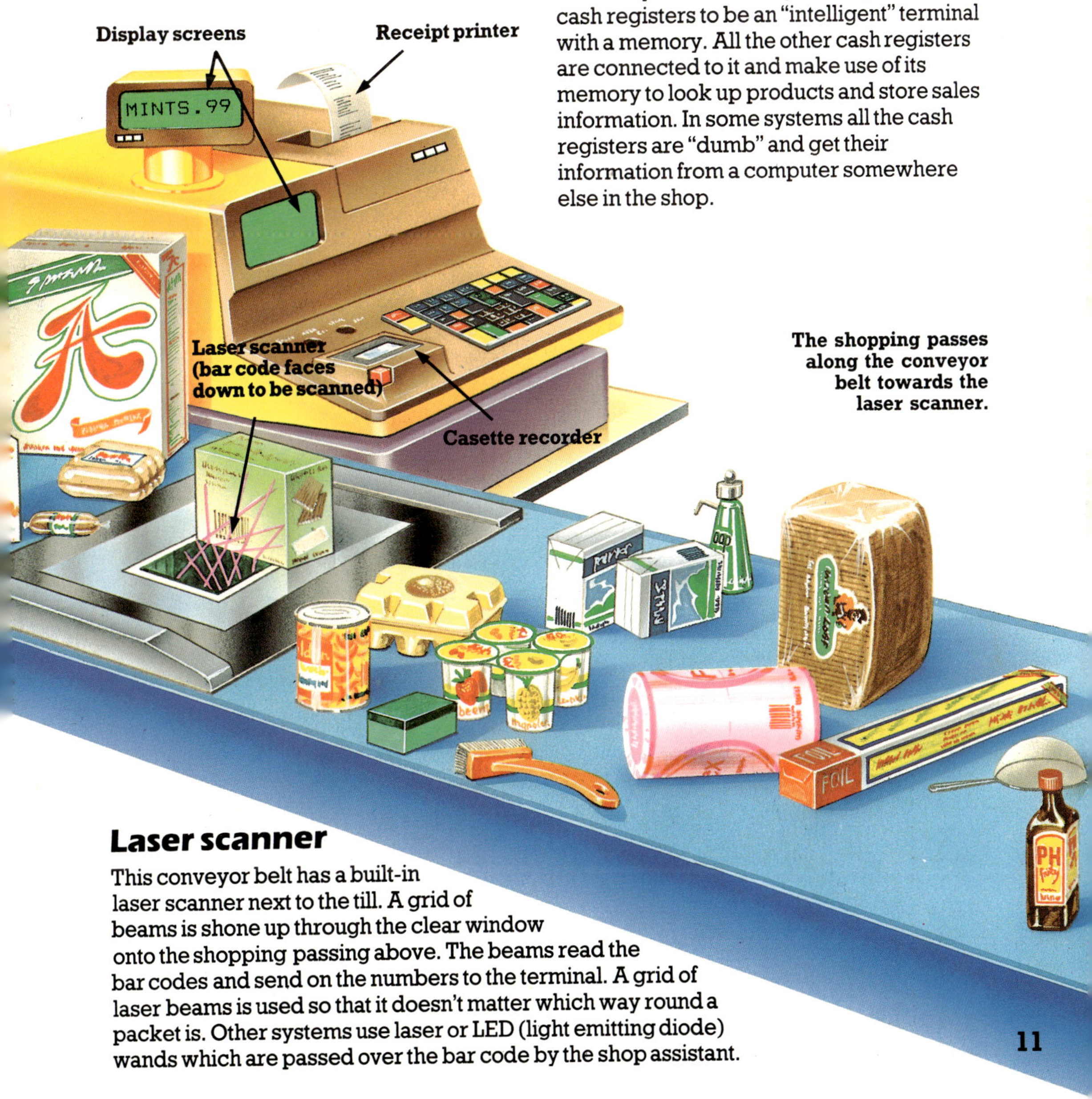

Display screens

Receipt printer

MINTS .99

Laser scanner (bar code faces down to be scanned)

Cassette recorder

The shopping passes along the conveyor belt towards the laser scanner.

Laser scanner

This conveyor belt has a built-in laser scanner next to the till. A grid of beams is shone up through the clear window onto the shopping passing above. The beams read the bar codes and send on the numbers to the terminal. A grid of laser beams is used so that it doesn't matter which way round a packet is. Other systems use laser or LED (light emitting diode) wands which are passed over the bar code by the shop assistant.

11

Electronic banking

Banking is another everyday area which involves a great deal of information processing well suited to computers. Banks already use computers to keep track of customers' accounts and international money markets. They are now looking at electronic ways of replacing cash and cheques so that amounts can be transferred easily from one account to another. This is known as electronic funds transfer (EFT), or even "the cashless society". Computerized terminals are already being used for some credit card transactions.

Electronic funds transfer (EFT)

In the cashless society, plastic debit cards will take the place of cash and cheques. They are used with computerized banking terminals in shops, like the one shown below. The card is slotted into the terminal and electronically scanned. The shop assistant keys-in the price of the things that you are buying.

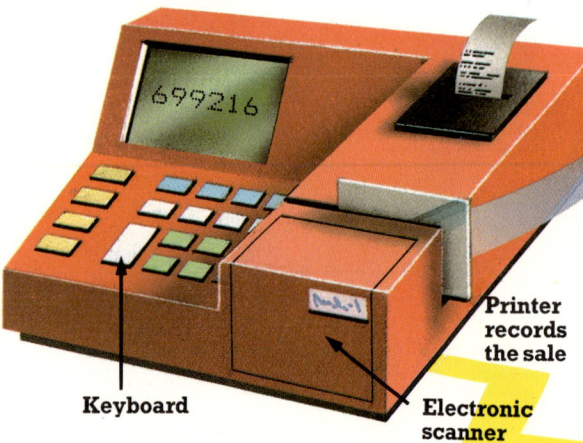

The debit card has your personal account number digitally encoded on the back so that it can be read directly by the terminal. The card above has the number recorded in three ways – as a magnetic stripe, a bar code and special printed characters that a computer can recognize. The terminal reads one or all of these to find out your number. (See pages 44 and 45 for how it is done.)

Some terminals just store details of debit card transactions on tape cassettes. These are later taken to the shop's bank and loaded into the main computer there for processing. The terminal pictured above, however, is an "on-line" communications machine, wired into the phone system. This means it calls the computer at the shop's bank automatically whenever a card is inserted and sends it details of the sale straight away.

The main computer at the shop's bank calls up, by phone, the computer at the customer's bank. It tells it the account number and the amount owed, instructing it to transfer the money to the shop's account.

Another kind of shop terminal can call up the main computer at the customer's bank to ask for payment itself, while the transaction is taking place.

When using a debit card you also have to key-in a personal identity number (PIN) on a separate keypad like the one above. This is linked to the terminal which checks your PIN against the number on the card as a security measure.

Cashpoint

PIN keypad

Printer

The first kind of electronic bank terminals were just automatic cash dispensers. These cashpoints are linked to the bank's main computer and allow you to take out cash, order cheque books and get a statement, using a plastic card. The main computer checks your card and PIN and if all is well tells the terminal to count out the money you want. There is a printer to print out a record of the transaction. Similar terminals are also used by the staff inside the bank to give them direct access to the main computer.

Memory cards

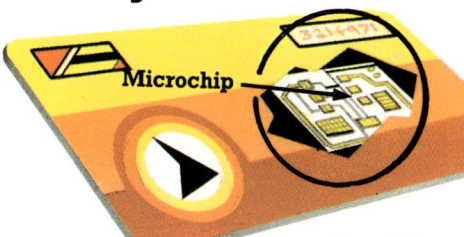

Microchip

These EFT cards have a tiny microchip embedded within the plastic. It records the amount of money in your bank account and then subtracts what you spend while using the card. When the card is put into a terminal the chip tells it to display your balance on the PIN keypad. If the terminal is on-line to the computer at your bank, the chip can find out if anything has been paid into your account and add it to its memory. It is also programmed to add and subtract regular payments like wages and rent automatically. These cards are sometimes called "intelligent" or "smart" cards.

Home telebanking

The most convenient kind of electronic banking is done at home using viewdata.* Your own computer is turned into a bank terminal when linked directly to your bank's computer by phone or cable TV. You can tell the bank to transfer money from your account to another, pay bills, and so on, electronically.

Transaction telephone

This telephone can make calls in the usual way, but it is also a banking terminal as it can scan and read the number on a credit card. The shop assistant uses the phone to call the computer at the credit card company and to scan the card. The phone itself passes the card number to the main computer, which checks that your account is not over its limit. If you are spending too much, the main computer automatically alerts the shop and passes the call to someone at the credit company. At the moment this is just a security check, but in the future EFT will allow the whole transaction to be automated and carried out electronically.

Credit card

*See page 16 for more about viewdata

TV technology

The information revolution is changing the way we use the TV – it can be a screen for home and distant computers, used for games, shopping, banking, watching films, communicating with other people and finding out information. Even ordinary TV programmes are reaching it in new ways. The TV set itself is changing too, making it more suitable for all these different functions and improving the quality of the pictures on the screen. Here are some of the developments that are taking place in TV technology.

Future TV

This picture shows a possible TV of the future with some of the extra things that will go with it. The set has a flat screen and is linked to hi-fi speakers for stereo sound. It is showing a cable channel that splits up the screen to show what is on the other channels. Some of the channels are interactive but the TV is also wired into the phone network to get viewdata*. This TV is also connected to a dish aerial for satellite broadcasts. There are video tape and disc players and a home computer, which use the TV's screen for display.

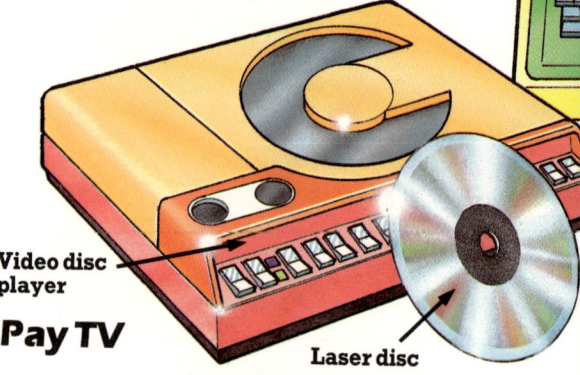

Pocket TV

Small, pocket TVs like those shown above are just being introduced. At the moment pocket TVs are the only ones with a flat screen. Some use liquid crystal displays (LCDs), like those used on calculators and watches. LCDs do not give a good enough picture for a large screen and only work in black and white.

Pay TV

Programmes broadcast from satellite and cable TV stations can be scrambled so that they can be seen only by people who have paid. For satellite sytems you will need to rent a decoder to unscramble the signals. With interactive cable systems the TV station can control which channels you see.

Satellite TV

TV stations have used satellites to send each other TV programmes for many years. The signals are beamed out to space and bounced off a satellite down to another part of Earth, where they are received by a dish aerial. The receiving TV station then transmits the signals to viewers in the usual way.

The latest development is direct broadcasting by satellite, known as DBS, where the signals go straight to the viewers. You need a special dish aerial, like the one shown here, to pick up DBS TV.

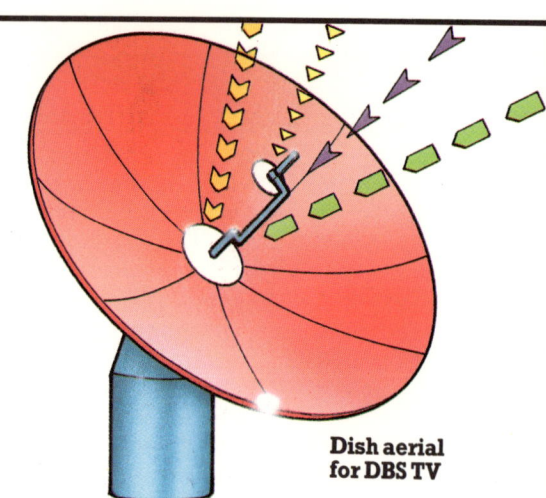

*You can find out more about viewdata on the next few pages.

Digital TV

At the moment TV is not recorded or broadcast using digital techniques. This is because a vast number of bits is required to carry the information of such detailed, moving pictures. The sound part is easy to digitize and so cable and satellite TV and video discs may use digital techniques to get better sound quality and stereo. Microchips inside the TV will decode the digital signals and reproduce the sound.

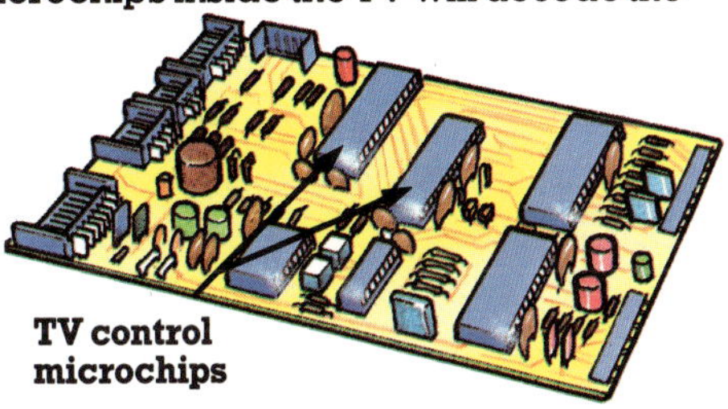

In fact, microchips are replacing many of the electronic components in TVs. They are already used for automatic channel tuning and remote control. Chips can be pre-programmed in the factory to memorize the best possible picture and then improve the image made from the signals they pick up. The picture is stored frame by frame and any interference, wobble, ghosting, wrong colour or brightness is corrected. As the picture is electronically stored by the TV, it will be possible for you to manipulate it in various ways – split the screen to show more than one channel, zoom into part of the picture, have freeze frames, slow motion and so on.

HD TV

A TV picture is made up from hundreds of rapidly changing lines. By increasing the number of lines used it is possible to get a more detailed picture. This is called high definition (HD) TV.

Cable TV

Cable has long been used to carry ordinary TV broadcasts to places where reception is poor or in blocks of flats to reduce the number of aerials. Now specialist cable TV channels that are not broadcast in the ordinary way are also becoming common. Cable can handle many more channels than ordinary broadcasting or even DBS. This allows specialist channels, devoted to just one subject such as sport, films, news or music, to be offered. This is sometimes called "narrowcasting" as it appeals to a smaller audience.

Cable can also be interactive if there is a direct cable line between all the viewers and the TV station. This allows viewers to respond to TV programmes – perhaps take part in quiz shows, question people being interviewed or vote on issues raised.

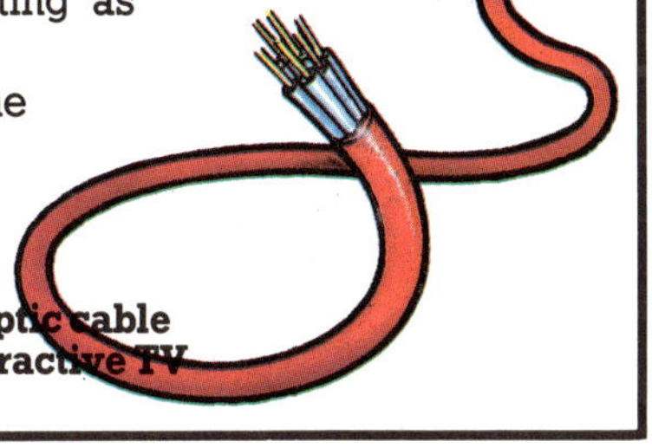

Information on your TV screen

Videotex turns your TV at home into the display screen for distant computers, giving you access to thousands of pages of useful information. You can use videotex to look-up the weather forecast, sports results, what's on at cinemas and theatres, travel timetables, get computer programs and discover facts about any number of topics.

There are two different types of videotex – viewdata and teletext. Both provide an electronic information service, but viewdata is a two-way communication system. With viewdata you can actually book a seat at the cinema or order goods, by sending a message back to the viewdata computer. This is impossible with teletext, as it is only one-way. This difference occurs because of the four ways that videotex can reach your TV, illustrated in the pictures below.

Broadcast TV: All TV signals broadcast over the air are one-way, so this method provides teletext.

Cable TV: Most cable TV channels are one-way, like ordinary TV, and so provide teletext.

Telephone: The telephone network is a two-way communication system and so provides viewdata.

Interactive cable TV: Some cable TV systems have special channels which allow viewers to send messages back to the TV station. They provide viewdata.

Finding a page

You call up videotex pages with a special remote control keypad or keyboard provided by the videotex company, or you may be able to use your home computer in some cases. A keypad has the numbers 0 to 9 and a few symbols such as * and # and possibly some commands such as "page store". A keyboard has the letters of the alphabet as well. If you know the number of the page you want to look at, you just key-in that number. Usually you don't know the number and so go through a series of menus which offer subjects to choose from. The menus get more and more specialized until you reach the pages with the information you want. It takes about five or six steps with viewdata, less for teletext as it has fewer pages. Some viewdata systems use a keyword search where you type in a word or phrase, such as "weather forecast", and the computer instantly finds the right pages for you. This is quicker than a menu choice, but you have to know what word or phrase to use.

Keypad

Keyboard

16

On the screen

Both viewdata and teletext provide information as screen-sized pages, sometimes called frames. The picture on the right shows part of a page in close up. Pages are made up of pictures (graphics) and writing (text) in bright colours. A page stays on the screen until you call up another, or switch off. Some adaptors have a microchip that memorizes the signals for one or more pages it has received and then displays them at your command.

How the image is made

The page is created from electronic signals sent out by the videotex computer. You have to have a special adaptor to decode these signals, so that they can be displayed on your TV screen. The image is formed on the screen by tiny squares called pixels, short for picture cells. The electronic signals tell a picture-generating chip in the decoder which pixels to light up and what colours they should be.

Graphics and text

Videotex graphics and text are square and simple looking. There is no sound and the only movement possible is a simple swapping of two images, rather like a flick-picture, as shown above. The footballer looks as if he is kicking the ball because two lots of pixels are being flashed on and off alternately.

Page information

The name of the videotex service usually appears at the top of the screen with the page number and some other information. Some services show the time and date, or the name of the organization which provides the information on that page.

Viewdata

Viewdata is the more useful kind of videotex as it is interactive, which means that you can send messages back to the viewdata computer. This central computer acts as an electronic post office, storing messages and passing them on to the right people. It also controls the databases full of pages of information. You can call up and look at this information but also respond to it – to do teleshopping, telebooking, telebanking, send electronic mail and so on. Viewdata can reach you by phone or two-way cable TV. These pages show how it works and what you need to be able to get it.

Registering

The first thing that you need to do is register as a subscriber with a viewdata service. You will get a user number, like a phone number, and a pass number or word. These give you access to the viewdata computers and databases.

Viewdata is not usually free. You may have to pay a joining fee, regular charges, computer and phone charges and even a fee for some of the pages, although most are free. You will also need some extra equipment, such as an adaptor, decoding software or modem and this may be provided when you join.

The screen

One thing you must have is a TV or monitor to be your viewdata display screen. It may have to be fitted with an adaptor that turns the signals reaching the TV back into text and graphics on the screen. The adaptor contains chips programmed to decode the viewdata signals and to generate the images by lighting up the right pixels on your TV screen.

Keypad

Interactive cable TV

As cable TV systems use cables that can actually link your TV set with the TV station, it is possible to send signals both ways. You will need an adaptor for the TV to decode the viewdata signals and generate the images. Not all cable TV channels are interactive, i.e. capable of being used for two-way communications. Cable TV viewdata is very new and so not widely used yet.

Keyboards

The viewdata organization may provide a keyboard or keypad. Keyboards are better as they have the alphabet and so you can write proper messages. With a keypad you can only make choices from an index or menu, such as the one below.

```
        Sending a greeting
           choose from
1...Happy birthday   3...Good luck
2...Valentine        4...Rude message
```

Viewdata by phone

This is the most common way of getting viewdata. In order to use the phone for computer communications of any kind, including viewdata, you need a modem – see below for what these are. The TV and phone are linked together via the modem, or the TV is linked directly to the phone line itself.

You telephone the viewdata computer, in the usual way, and it answers your call automatically. It displays a message on the screen, asking for your user number and pass word. Having logged on to the computer by giving it this data, you can call up pages, send messages and so on. The viewdata computer monitors your call, gets the pages you ask for from the database, sends them to you and deals with all the other people using the service too.

This picture shows a TV and phone set up to get viewdata, using an acoustic coupler modem. There is a keypad, a keyboard and a home computer too.

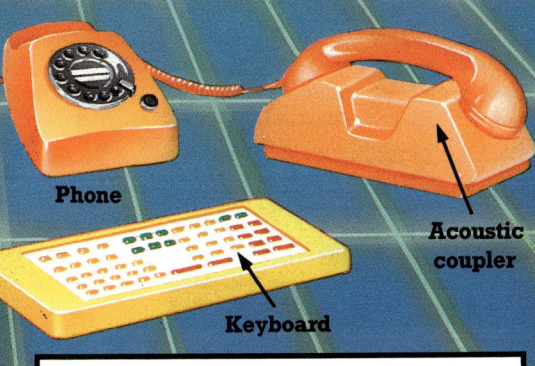

Phone

Acoustic coupler

Keyboard

What is a modem?

A modem is a device that converts computer data into a signal that can be sent over the phone and back again. There are several kinds of modem. One sort called an acoustic coupler is shown in the main picture on this page. The handset of your phone fits into two cups on the coupler and it converts the sounds coming out of the earpiece into electrical signals that the adaptor in the TV, or the computer, can use. It also changes the things you type into noises and feeds them into the phone's mouthpiece. Outside noises can interfere with reception when using an acoustic

Phone

Direct coupler

coupler so that a lot of garbled letters and symbols appear on the screen.

A better kind of modem, called a direct coupler, is actually connected to the phone line. This means that it gets the phone signals as electricity from the line and you don't have to use the handset. The phone pictured above is standing on a modem of this kind. You need a special socket fitted to your phone line to plug the modem into. Some TV adaptors and computers contain modem microchips and they can also be plugged into these special sockets.

Viewdata and home computers

If you have a home computer you may be able to use it as a keyboard. It will also act as a decoder and image generator, so you will not need an adaptor for the TV. You will need some special software to make your computer understand the viewdata's coded signals.

Computer

19

The viewdata computers and databases

Databases used to store information

Computer

The TV and phone are the user's end of the viewdata system, but at its heart are the central computers and databases. The computers are large, powerful machines, able to organize the flow of very large amounts of information in and out of the databases. The databases are machines that hold all the pages of information, stored electronically on magnetic disks.

Information providers

The information in the databases of many general viewdata systems is not actually put together by the viewdata service. They provide the computing power, equipment and sometimes telecommunications but sell space in the databases to organization such as governments, shops, banks, airlines, newspapers, businesses – in fact anyone who wants it. These information providers (IPs) make up their pages on microcomputers like the one on the right and send them to the central database, by phone. Electronically stored information can be updated instantly, which is very useful for information that is always changing.

Microcomputer

Private pages

An IP can instruct the viewdata computer to allow only certain people to see some of their pages. This is called a closed user group (CUG). The computer is given the user numbers of all the people in the CUG and will then deny access to anyone else. This facility is used by companies with country-wide branches and scattered staff to provide electronic communications. Some CUGs can be joined by anyone, for a fee, and provide useful things like telesoftware computer programs.

Gateways

Lots of organizations have their own large computers and vast databases of information. These can be linked up with the viewdata network so that subscribers have direct access to them. This is sometimes called a gateway. Banks use computers a lot and with a viewdata gateway you can look up your account and instruct the computer to make payments. This is known as telebanking. You can even use viewdata to look at the arrival and departure indicator boards in an airport, if they are generated on a computer linked to the network.

1	PARIS	14	10:15
2	LONDON	17	12:55
3	NEW YORK	6	11:40
4	FRANKFURT	9	DELAYED
5		12	10:25
			10:15
			14:16

Airport indicator board

Database

Specialist services

Not all viewdata services provide general information. Some specialize in one subject only of interest to a particular group – such as medical information for doctors, legal facts for lawyers and details of travel and holidays for travel agents.

Viewdata future

Viewdata technology and communications links could also be used for other things as well as ordinary viewdata. It could provide the basis of many of the services described in the cabled city.

If the phone line is linked by a special socket to the mains electricity of a house, it is possible for equipment to be controlled over the phone. The gas, electricity and other meters could be read over the phone by computers at the electricity or gas office.

It may also be possible to have a central, computer-controlled library of video discs that you could call up and choose from over cable TV, just like pages of videotex. Viewphones, where you see on your TV the person you are talking to on the phone, are another possibility for the future.

21

Teletext

Teletext is another kind of videotex that brings screen-sized pages of information to your TV from a central computer. Teletext is broadcast on TV channels at the same time as ordinary TV programs and picked up by your TV in the usual way. You need a special teletext adaptor to decode and display the digital teletext signals. Some TVs have a decoder already fitted, or you can buy one to adapt an old TV. You also need a remote control teletext keypad, like the one below, to call up pages you want.

As teletext is broadcast, it is a one-way only system, unlike viewdata. In fact it differs from viewdata in several ways, which are explained on these two pages.

Transmitting teletext

Teletext pages are made up and stored electronically by computers similar to those used for viewdata. Teletext services usually have fewer pages than viewdata – just a few hundred rather than thousands. The pages are broadcast one after another as a continuous stream and it takes a couple of minutes to send out the whole lot. Once they have all been broadcast the cycle starts again. This means that the pages are not all available at the same time, as on viewdata. You will have to wait for the one you want to be broadcast. This is usually only a few seconds, but it depends upon the total number of pages and whether you have just missed it. Popular pages appear more than once in a cycle. Teletext pages are numbered and you choose what you want to see from menus and call it up with the keypad.

These keys are used for controlling the teletext pages.

These keys control the TV channel selection.

A teletext keypad like this instructs the TV to switch from ordinary programmes to teletext. Most remote control keypads work by sending out instructions coded by a beam of infra-red light. An infra-red receiver in the TV set picks up and decodes these instructions and passes them on to the teletext adaptor.

The symbols control the special functions that teletext offers, which are shown on the right. A page remains unchanged on the screen once it has been displayed.

In Britain the BBC's teletext is called Ceefax, the ITV's is called Oracle.

Teletext signals

All TV pictures are made up of hundreds of horizontal lines which change many times a second to produce the familiar moving pictures on the screen. There are a few spare lines, which are not used for the normal TV image, at the top and bottom of the screen. The top lines are used for teletext signals, the bottom ones carry information for TV engineers at the transmitters. On a badly tuned TV, where the picture has slipped and the top spare lines show, you can see the digital code of teletext signals as a series of rapidly changing bright dots. These tell the microchips in the adaptor what to display to make a page. The microchips wait for the page you want, store the signals that form it and then display the page on the screen.

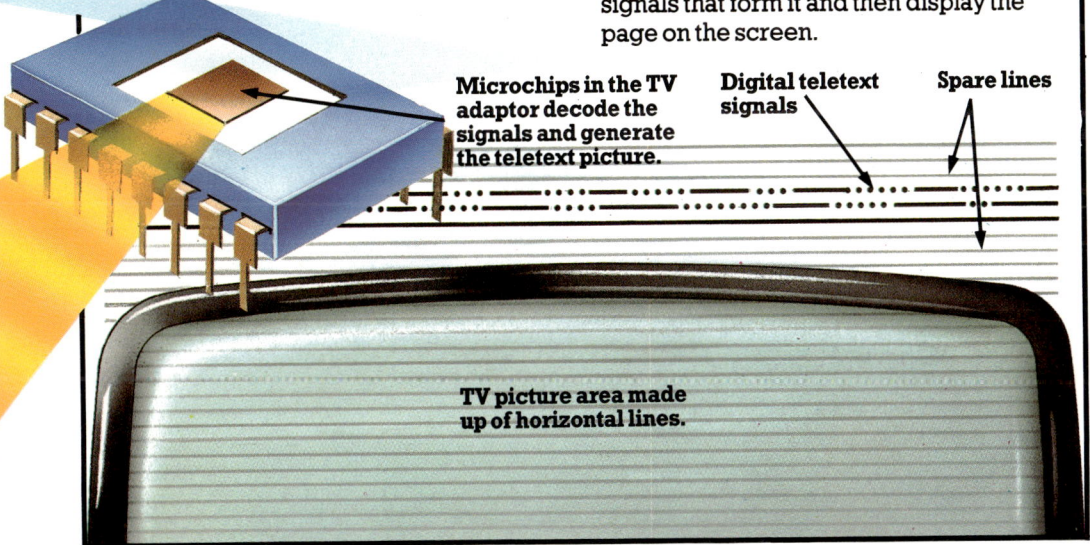

Microchips in the TV adaptor decode the signals and generate the teletext picture.

Digital teletext signals

Spare lines

TV picture area made up of horizontal lines.

What's on teletext

Like viewdata, teletext provides lots of useful information such as news, sports results, weather, recipes, travel guides, puzzles and so on. Although there is less information than on viewdata and it is not interactive, teletext does have some advantages. It is free, apart from the cost of an adaptor. Also, as the teletext is being continuously broadcast on the

same channel as TV programmes and at the same time, it has some features that viewdata does not. Teletext can be mixed with an ordinary programme to give sub-titles on the screen in time with the pictures. The adaptor can be programmed to display a certain page at a particular time, an airport's timetable when you are awaiting a plane to arrive, for example. You can also ask for a page to appear as soon as it is updated, say to get a news flash like the one above.

Telesoftware

If you have a home computer, you need programs to run on it. Telesoftware is a new, very convenient way of getting computer programs, via videotex. The software is loaded directly into your computer. It can reach you as broadcast teletext signals or as viewdata, either by interactive cable TV or phone line. Telesoftware is much easier than typing long programs from magazines and can be cheaper than buying cassettes.

Getting telesoftware

Telesoftware programs are written as pages of text, stored in the videotex company's database and transmitted just like any other kind of videotex information. Teletext telesoftware is broadcast, viewdata telesoftware is sent down the phone line or via cable TV.

You may need some extra equipment, such as an adaptor or modem, in order to pick up videotex. Some special software that enables your computer to understand the videotex code may also be necessary.

Telesoftware services often provide much more than just programs – pages of computer and software news, reviews, hints, letters, advertisements and puzzles for instance. You may have to pay for some programs and for the telesoftware service itself if it reaches you as pay TV or phone viewdata. Teletext is usually free.

Teletext telesoftware

Teletext telesoftware usually has fewer programs available than viewdata and they will probably be shorter. You need a special adaptor/receiver, which you connect to your computer, to pick up the teletext signals. This is because if you are using your TV as the display screen for your home computer, it will be tuned to the channel that the computer uses. The TV cannot receive the teletext channel at the same time, so you need another receiver to do this. The adaptor also decodes the teletext signals so you do not need a special teletext TV or extra software. Another reason for having a separate adaptor/receiver is because the TV cannot feed the teletext information into the computer.

Cable software

If the telesoftware is part of an interactive cable TV service, it is likely to be on a pay-channel that is devoted to viewdata. You must pay to see the channel, as well as for the software you want. You may need a special adaptor fitted to your TV so that it can pick up the signals and send them to your computer, as well as some software to allow your computer to decode these signals.

One day it may even be possible to use telesoftware via viewdata without even having your own computer. The central viewdata computers could run programs for you, displaying the results like ordinary pages for you to control with the teletext keypad.

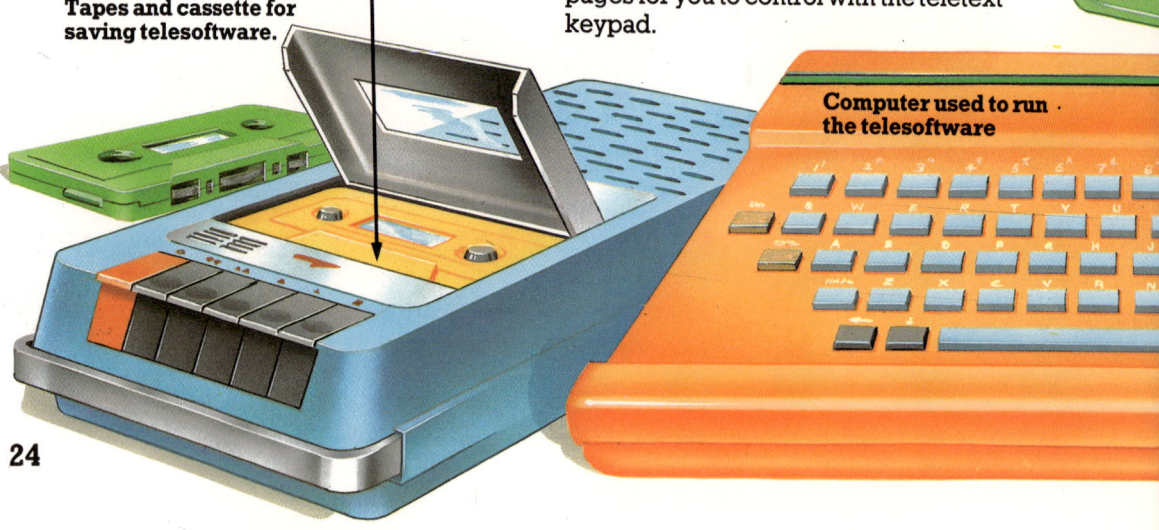

This software programs your computer to decode the teletext signals.

Tapes and cassette for saving telesoftware.

Computer used to run the telesoftware

Software by phone

To get telesoftware from a phone viewdata service you need to be set up to receive viewdata, as described on pages 18 and 19. Telesoftware by phone is likely to be provided by a closed user group that has rented space in the viewdata database. Once you have joined to get telesoftware you will be able to get the other viewdata services too. The picture below shows a home computer receiving a games program over the phone, using an acoustic coupler modem.

TV used as a display screen for telesoftware

Downloading telesoftware

Putting telesoftware into your computer is called downloading. You choose programs that you want from menus. They are usually grouped by subject, such as games, business, education and so on, but even more importantly by kind of computer. This is because programs written for one computer will not run on another kind. Computer programs are written in special computer languages, usually BASIC or machine code for home computers. Unfortunately different kinds of computer use different versions of BASIC and machine code, so you will only be able to download software written for your type of computer.

While it is downloading, a program may appear on your TV screen as lines of words, letters and symbols, which often look like rubbish. This is because programs are transmitted in a special compacted code that is shorter and therefore faster to send than ordinary computer languages. Once the program is loaded you can run it, store it on tape or disk for future use, display it on the screen or print it out if you want to see it written down.

Phone and acoustic coupler modem

The electronic office

Most office work involves dealing with information written down on pieces of paper. When it is not being processed by people, this paper is filed away for future reference. This is not a particularly easy or fast way of dealing with information – a computerized system can be much more efficient. The office of the future is sometimes called "the paperless office" as all the information is stored electronically. These pages look at some of the changes that are taking place now.

Data links

✱ As all the work stations are linked together they can be used for electronic mail. You can send memos and letters to anyone else in the office, even to everyone at once.

✱ The work stations have a calender/diary for you to record all your appointments. You can arrange meetings with other people electronically, using your terminal to scan

Work stations

In the electronic office people will work at computerized work stations, like the one shown below. It is made up of a microcomputer keyboard, visual display unit (VDU) and a telephone. Several work stations may share other equipment such as printers and intelligent photocopiers. All the work stations in the office are linked together and to a central computer and database of information.

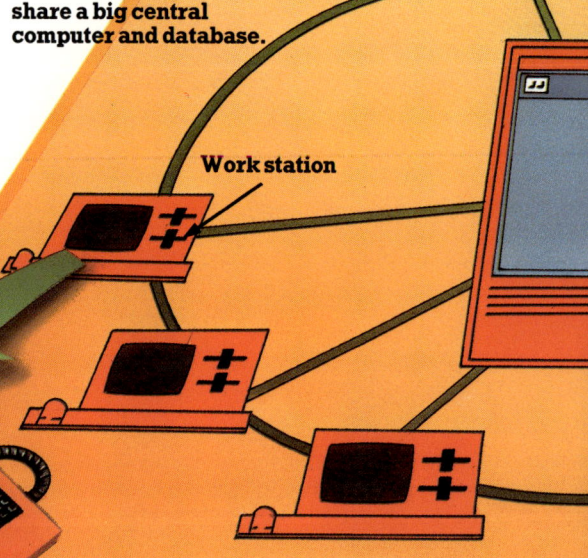

This diagram shows how several work stations can be linked together as a network. They all share a big central computer and database.

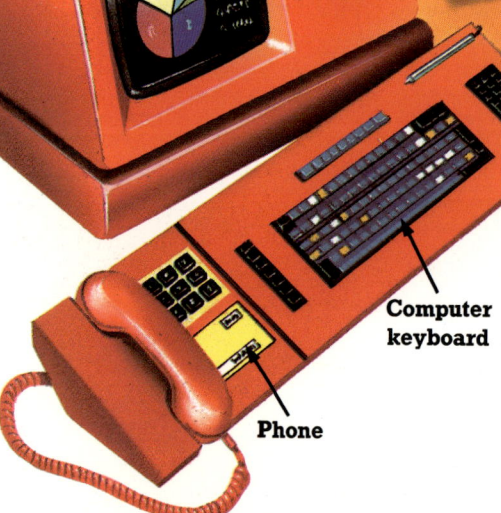

As work stations can easily be linked by phone it is possible for people to have their work station at home. The office of the future may be an electronic network rather than a building.

Networking

Communications are vital to the electronic office. The work stations in a single building will be linked together by cables to form a network. This enables information to be passed between people electronically, say for approval or further processing. The receiving work station can store the data or alert its user, depending upon the priority rating given to the message. A work station phone has a built-in modem so that computer data can be transmitted easily outside the office. With satellite links, a company in America can send data direct to its European office in seconds.

the diaries of the people you want to meet to see when they are all free.

✱ You can also send electronic voice messages over the phone. The receiving work station records your voice digitally and plays it back as a commentary to go with information on the screen.

✱ Every work station has access to the same database of information but can run its own program to deal with it in different ways.

Working with computers

As work stations are computers you can run programs which help with your work. Computers can manipulate information very fast, doing in a few seconds things that would be impossible without the help of a computer.

Word processing programs make writing and changing documents much easier (see pages 28 and 29). Other programs automatically work out things like the wages – printing out individual payslips and transferring the right amount of money for every member of staff. Modelling programs allow you to work out what would happen if various things change in different ways in relation to each other.

The electronic office also automates many of the routine jobs like re-typing standard documents and addressing mail, as computers can be programmed to control other electronic machines. Even familiar office equipment such as photocopiers and telex machines can be controlled by computer and improved by microelectronics.

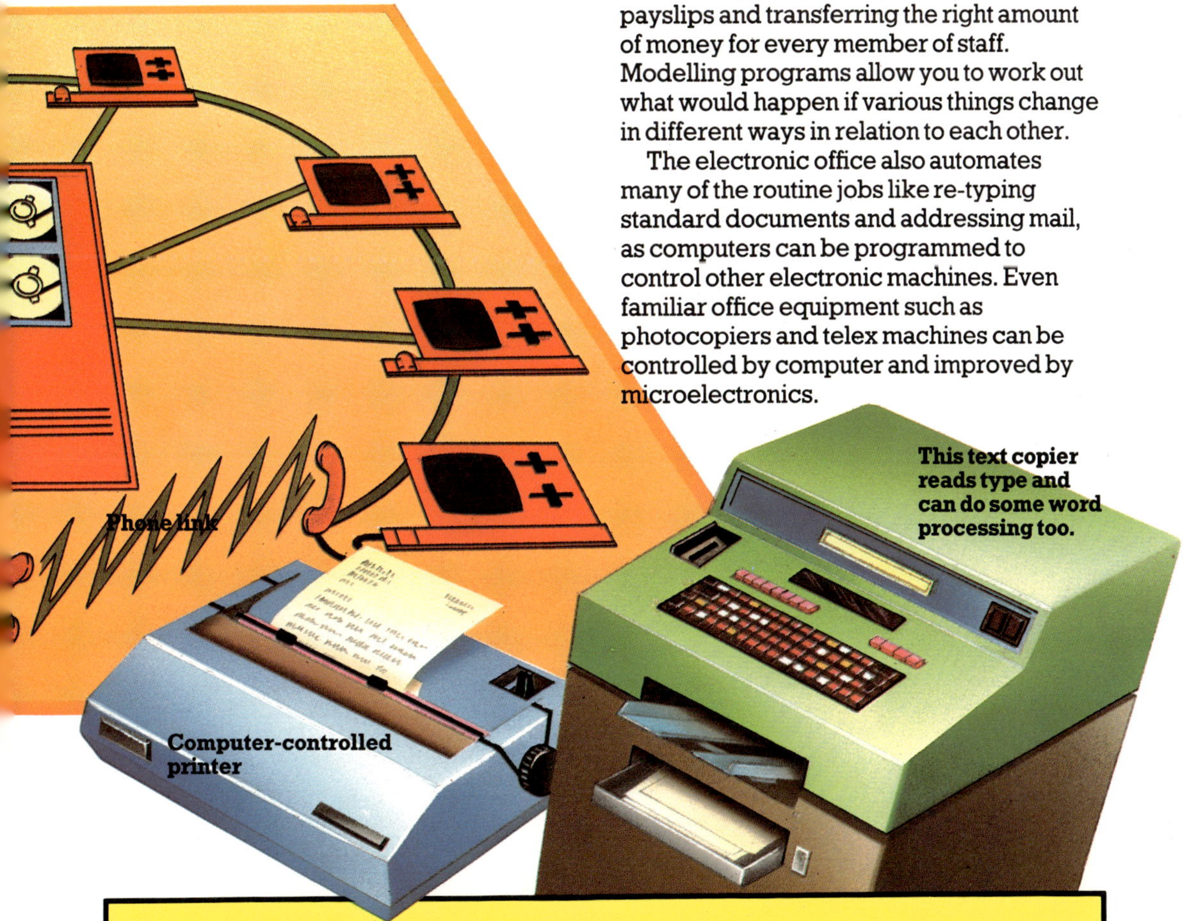

Phone link

Computer-controlled printer

This text copier reads type and can do some word processing too.

Machines that "read" and "write"

Even in the electronic office information will still need to be put on paper sometimes, so machines that can automatically read text for storage or reproduction are very useful. They save having to re-type or word process written documents if there is just a small change to be made. The picture above shows a machine that can read type and be programmed to change parts of a document before making copies of it. The other machine is a computer-controlled printer which can type a page of text in seconds.

Word processing

Word processors are revolutionizing writing in the same way that electronic calculators have already affected arithmetic. They are computers designed to make the manipulation of text quick and easy. With a word processor you can electronically edit what you have written, completely changing the layout, order of words and sentences and even replace words without having to re-type the whole thing.

This picture shows a dedicated computer which cannot do anything but word processing. Dedicated machines like this have a keyboard with special keys that control the editing and other functions, to make them easier to use. You can also buy word processing programs on disk, tape or chip to run with an ordinary computer.

Using a word processor

Your text is displayed on the VDU as you type it in at the keyboard. You can make changes and corrections as you go along, using the editing keys and a movable pointer, called the cursor, to tell the word processor what to change. The text is stored inside the word processor's memory, as well as being displayed, so you can go back over it later. You can also store it permanently on disk, or tape, for reference or later editing. A word processor has to be connected to an electronic printer in order to produce a typed copy of your text stored in its memory. It takes a little time to learn to use a word processor as they can do so many things. Here are some of the main functions.

Word search

Global search is a useful command which automatically searches for and replaces a particular word, every time it occurs anywhere in the text. For example if you have just finished your 80,000 word novel "The life of Tiddles" and decide to change the hero's name to Bonzo, the word processor will look at all 80,000 words and replaces every Tiddles with Bonzo, instantly. You can also search selectively, with the word processor stopping every time it finds the word so that you can decide whether to change it.

Editing

After writing your text you will probably want to edit it, to get rid of mistakes and make changes. With an ordinary typewriter this would mean a lot of re-typing but with a word processor you can do it electronically before printing. You can remove any words and the word processor will automatically close up the space left, repositioning the rest of the paragraph too. Inserting extra words is also easy and the word processor readjusts the rest of the text to fit them in. An overwriting function lets you replace unwanted words with new ones. The word processor will also move parts of the text around if you want to change the order but not the words.

Page design

You have to tell the word processor how to arrange the text that you are writing. Once you have specified the line length and spacing, indentations, margins, headings, pages and so on you are ready to type. The machine automatically lays out the text when it is printed. If a word is too long to fit on the end of a line the word processor takes it down to the next, on screen as well as when printed.

Words on a chip

Until recently, most word processors were large office machines. Now you can buy a word processing program permanently stored on a microchip to fit in your home computer. It will not do as much as an office machine but should do the things mentioned here.

Extra programs

Additional programs are available on disk to help you improve your writing. A spelling program compares every word in your text to the thousands of words it has stored as a dictionary on disk. If it finds a word not in the dictionary, the word processor highlights it on the screen for you to check your spelling or typing and correct any errors.

If you are stuck for a good word you can use a thesaurus program to supply synonyms (words of similar meaning) to the one you indicate. Another program will even check your grammar against rules stored on disk and suggest changes for you to insert. It is even possible to have a program to improve your English. This will suggest simpler ways of putting things if you have been too wordy, as illustrated here on the screen and picture above.

Microwriter

This is a Microwriter. It is an electronic word processor but does not have a standard keyboard. Instead you press a combination of its six keys to produce all the letters of the alphabet, numbers, symbols and to give the Microwriter special commands. Your text moves across the one line display and is stored inside the machine. You can edit and correct with a Microwriter and also link it to other electronic machines such as TVs, word processors, computers, printers, cassettes and modems for further text editing, processing, printing, storage and communications. It is rather like a "word calculator".

Future phones

Microelectronic technology is enabling the phone to do much more than just make and receive calls. The telephone of tomorrow will be more useful than the one you use today. In fact many of these developments are available already but are not yet very common. Here are some of the things that you can expect to find being added to your phones over the next few years.

Making connections

Display screen shows numbers and messages

Command keys for programming the phone

Phones will be fitted with special sockets so that they can be connected to electronic machines, like printers, computers and TVs, that need telecommunications links. They will also have built-in modems for data transmission.

Directory enquiries

With the phone of the future you will not need a pile of thick telephone directories full of numbers that you will never want to know. Instead, all directories will be electronically stored on a computer database and you will make enquiries over the phone using a kind of viewdata. A computerized system will be much faster than an operator and will even be able to find numbers if you are not sure of the spelling of a name or just know the address.

Programmable phones

Telephones will contain microchips programmed to carry out various functions, like the ones listed here, at your command. The keyboard will have the usual numbers and some special programming keys too, possibly even an alphabetic keyboard.
Automatic calling: The phone will memorize frequently used numbers and automatically call them in response to a single digit code.
Call bar: You will be able to program your phone to stop any calls being made either to or from your phone, say while you are on holiday.
Re-routing: If you are going to be at another number you can get your phone to transfer your calls to it.
Repeat call: The phone will keep trying a number that is busy and let you know when it has got through.
Voice messages: These are digitally recorded messages. Chips will be able to play messages to people and record their messages while you are out.

Display screen

The built-in display screens will show the number that you call so that you can see if you have made a mistake and also display the cost as you are speaking, or at the end of a call. It can also show the number of a phone making an incoming call so that you can see who it is before answering... or not. The display will also tell you if someone is calling your number while you are on the phone or have barred in-coming calls.

Number keys

Speech synthesis

Phones will contain chips that speak to your callers when you can't. They will be ready programmed to tell someone who is trying to call you if their call is being re-routed to another phone or, that the line is busy.

Computerized phone exchanges will also use speech synthesis to give callers information, automatically. The computer will monitor a call, work out the cost and pass this data to the speech chips to say.

Radio telephones

Short range mobile phone

A phone does not have to be at the end of a cable but can work with radio waves too. In fact lots of phone calls travel as radio waves now. Some long distance and all satellite links are made by microwave – a kind of radio.

Short range cordless phones, like the one above, use an adaptor fitted to your ordinary phone. This converts the electrical waves of incoming calls into radio waves and broadcasts them to the mobile radio phone. Speaking into the radio phone produces radio waves that are picked up by the adaptor and sent down the phone line in the usual way.

Cellular systems

Short range radio phones only work with an adaptor on an ordinary phone and can cover only a small area. Completely radio networks can work over long distances and do not need a connection with the ordinary phone lines at all. They work by having an overlapping network of computer-controlled radio transmitters. Each one covers a small zone, known as a cell, and calls are routed through cells until they reach the one that the receiving phone is in. This sort of system allows phones to be mobile as the computers pass your call from one cell to another as you move around between them.

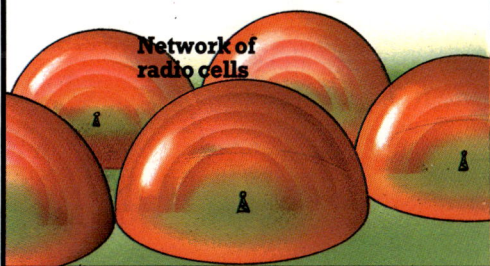

Network of radio cells

31

What does "telecommunications" mean?

The word telecommunications means communication over a long distance. Broadcasting TV and radio signals is one form of telecommunication, but the main two-way telecommunications system in use today is the telephone network. It was designed and set up to transmit voices so that people could speak to each other. The information revolution depends upon good communications between computers. Services such as viewdata, teleshopping, electronic banking, the electronic office and so on cannot work without good telecommunications links. Phone networks are being redeveloped to make computer communication easier.

How phones work now

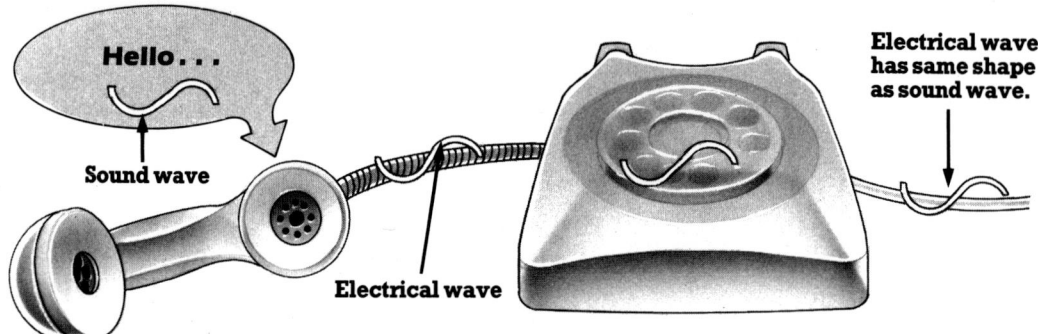

When you speak your voice produces a sound wave in the air. This is turned into an electrical wave by a microphone inside the mouthpiece of your phone. The electrical wave representing your voice travels along cables in the phone network, through exchanges which route it in the right direction, to the receiving phone. At this phone's earpiece, the electrical wave is converted back into a sound wave, recreating your voice. This sort of system is called analogue transmission, as the electrical wave is analogous (similar) to the sound wave.

Facsimile transmission

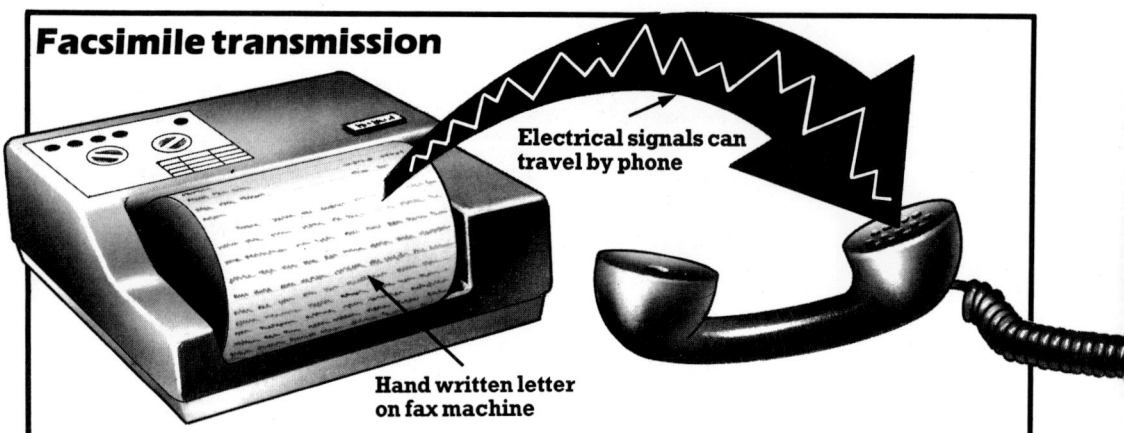

Telephones and computers are not the only machines that can communicate by phone lines. This is a facsimile (fax) machine, which can send and receive any kind of document — printed or hand written text, painted or photographed pictures. They work by scanning the document, reading the degree of lightness and darkness all over the page. These values are converted into electrical signals that can be sent through the phone system. The receiving machine, which is called up like a phone, decodes the electrical signals and prints out a facsimile (exact copy) of the original. Other kinds of telecommunications machines with keyboards, can send and receive typed messages over the phone.

Digital phone systems

Computers work with digital signals not analogue, so when they communicate by phone their data has to be converted by a modem at both ends. Computer communication would be much easier if the phone system worked digitally and could transmit computer data without converting it. Many phone networks are being changed so that they can deal directly with digital data and some are already partly digital. In this kind of system, voices need to be "digitized" for the journey. This picture shows how it is done.

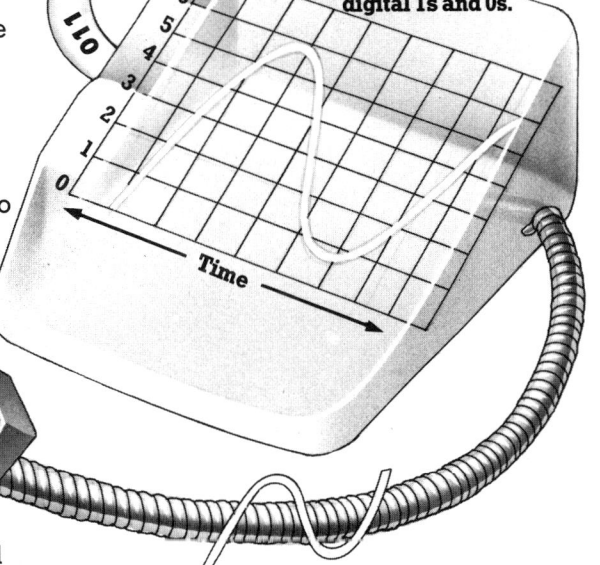

Electrical wave representing your voice is measured and turned into digital 1s and 0s.

Your voice wave is turned into an electrical wave, as in the ordinary analogue telephone system. The wave is measured thousands of times a second, giving a series of numbers which represent its height at different times. These numbers are converted into binary digital data – on/off bits – which can be transmitted as pulses through the phone system. At the other end, the bits are converted back into the sound of your voice.

Computer exchanges

Even though the phone system is not yet completely digital, exchanges which route calls through the network are being computerized. These can handle more information, more quickly than the old mechanical exchanges so there should be fewer misconnections, crossed lines, interference and lost calls. Computer-controlled exchanges can also offer extra services such as re-routing calls to another phone, viewdata phone number directories, automatic monitoring of calls and voice synthesis for passing on routine information such as the cost of calls or messages about busy lines.

Fibre optic cables

At the moment most phone calls travel as electricity along copper cables but they can also be sent as light along thin strands of glass called optical fibres. The advantage of optical fibres is that they can carry much more information than copper cables. This picture shows a bundle of optical fibres capable of transmitting 10,000 telephone calls, compared with the copper cables necessary. Another advantage of fibre optics is that the phone line cannot be tapped.

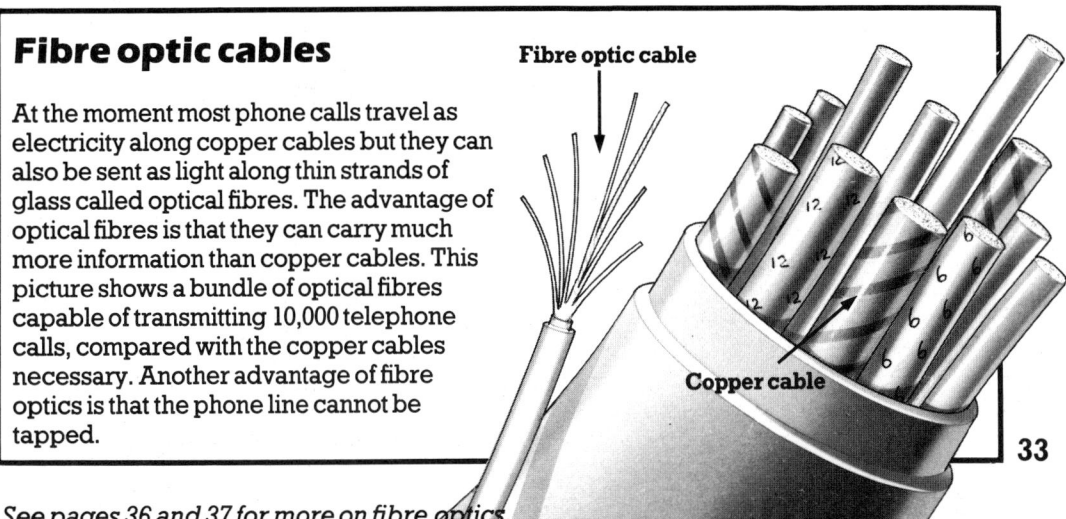

See pages 36 and 37 for more on fibre optics.

Satellite Communications

Telecommunications messages are not only broadcast and sent along phone cables, but also beamed out into space and bounced off satellites. Every day thousands of phone calls, TV signals and streams of computer data travel from one side of the world to the other in seconds via satellites.

Communications satellites can handle more information than cables and also transmit it much faster. Computer data that would take all day to send by phone could reach its destination in just a quarter of an hour by satellite.

Sending signals

Information is beamed to and from satellites as microwave signals, which are a kind of short radio wave that can travel through space. The signals are sent and received by dish-shaped aerials called earth stations. When satellite communication was first developed, aerials had to be huge. Now

This dish aerial on the roof of the *Financial Times* building in central London was used experimentally to beam the paper to a printer in Germany.

they are small enough to be installed in a car park or on a roof, like the one shown here. America's national newspaper *USA Today* is only possible because a satellite can transmit it directly to newspaper offices all over the country where it can be printed and distributed locally.

Satellite orbits

A telecommunications satellite must be in the same place in the sky all the time, so that the earth stations can be pointed towards it. This will only happen when a satellite is 35,800km (22,300mi) above the equator. This is called a geosynchronous orbit. In this orbit a satellite takes exactly the same time to orbit the earth as the Earth takes to rotate once on its axis

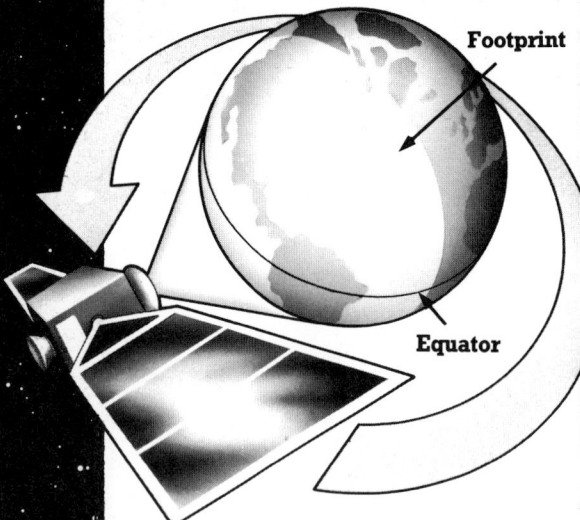

(23hrs 56mins). The satellite is always above the same place on Earth and seems to hover motionless in the sky. One satellite can cover only about 40% of the Earth and the area that it covers is known as its footprint.

Using satellites

You will need your own small dish aerial if you want to get TV broadcast by satellite – known as DBS. Even without your own aerial you can still use communication satellites, via the ordinary phone network. You have probably sent your voice by satellite if you have ever made a very long distance phone call.

Direct satellite links could be useful for multinational organizations – all their offices round the world could be linked together, office work stations could communicate with each other, central databases be accessed by terminals on another continent, or a central computer could send new instructions to a robot thousands of kilometres away and so on.

At the satellite

The satellite picks up the signals with small dish-shaped aerials and then transmits them back to a different part of Earth. It also boosts the signals, making them easier for small aerials to receive. Signals from a satellite can be picked up by any suitable aerial in its footprint.

Dish aerials

Information that needs to be kept secret, such as computer data, has to be coded or scrambled before transmission. An aerial can pick up signals from all the satellites whose footprints cover it.

Only the very newest satellites can handle digital data. The older ones use analogue techniques and so are slower and transmit less information. Newer satellites are bigger too and can boost the signal so much that even tiny aerials, like those used for DBS TV, can receive the signals.

There are over 170 telecommunications satellites in space already and several more are planned to be launched over the next few years. Some will be dedicated to data transmission or DBS TV instead of general telecommunications. The geosynchronous orbit is getting so crowded that neighbouring satellites have to use different radio frequencies to stop interference between signals.

Picking up signals

Most satellite signals cannot be picked up by ordinary radios but only by the special dish-shaped aerials. The signals are so weak they have to be concentrated together by the dish of the aerial. The microwaves hit the inside of the dish and are all bounced to the same place, just above the middle of the dish. This is the focus point. The aerial has to be tuned, as different messages are transmitted at different frequencies, just like ordinary radio. Dishes must also be carefully positioned to get signals from particular satellites.

The aerial turns the radio signals it picks up into electricity. This is sent, by wire, to the receiving machine, which could be a TV, telephone exchange, computer or whatever, and decoded back into its original form.

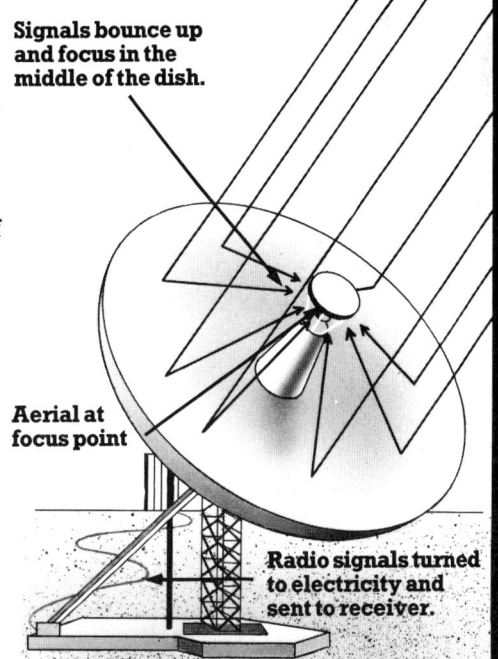

Signals bounce up and focus in the middle of the dish.

Aerial at focus point

Radio signals turned to electricity and sent to receiver.

35

Fibre optics

At the moment most telecommunications links for phones, cable TV, computers and so on are made with copper cables which carry messages as electricity. Optical fibres are a new kind of communications cable that use light rather than electricity. They will probably become widely used in the future as they can carry more TV channels or phone calls in a single cable than copper cables can. Optical fibres are also better suited to the two-way, interactive links needed for viewdata and other computer communications. They are already being used by telephone companies but are not yet very common, as ordinary copper cabling is usually cheaper.

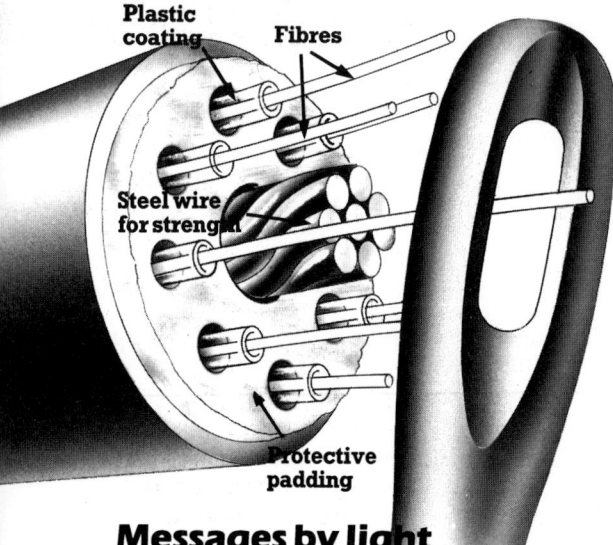

Channelling light

Light was not used for telecommunications in the past as there was no way of channelling it from place to place. It cannot be broadcast like radio waves or travel along metal wires like electricity. It was the invention of optical fibres in the 1960s that provided a channel. Optical fibres are tubes of glass (or sometimes plastic), stretched as thin as hair, like the ones shown here. The fibres are completely flexible and can be bent and twisted like wire. They are used bundled together to form cables. Light can travel along a fibre in a continuous beam, or as digital on/off pulses.

Messages by light

Light is just one part of the electromagnetic spectrum, pictured below, which includes radio waves. We are used to the idea of radio waves carrying information to our TVs and radios but light can do this too. In fact it can transmit more information than radio.

Radio waves	**Micro waves**	**Infra-red**	**Visible light**	**Ultra-violet**	**X-rays**	**Gamma-rays**

All electromagnetic radiation takes the form of waves. The waves are measured in length – the distance between waves – and frequency – the number of waves a second. Different kinds of waves have different lengths and frequencies. The shorter the wavelength, the higher its frequency. It is rather like comparing a giant's footsteps with a dwarf's. In one second a giant can make one long step, a dwarf takes lots of little ones. Light has a very much shorter wavelength than radio. Millions of light waves can fit into a single millimetre, but a single radio wave can be thousands of metres long. This means that light has more waves a second which can be used to carry information and so can transmit a greater amount than radio can, in the same time.

This diagram is not to scale

How optical fibres work

Optical fibres are made from glass so clear and pure that a sheet 35km thick would be as transparent as an ordinary window pane. Light does not leak out of the fibres because they have an outer cladding of different glass. This makes the light bounce back into the very pure core at the centre, as illustrated here. The light travels along the fibre bouncing from side to side.

The most modern, and expensive, kind of optical fibres have a carefully graded cladding and an extremely thin core that keep the light in a straight line. These are used with lasers, the only light source to produce a parallel beam.

Light sources

As optical fibres are so thin, the light source used to flash light into them must be tiny too. Small light-emitting diodes (LEDs) or laser "chips" are used. LEDs are electronic devices which produce a light when they receive an electric current. Laser chips are made from tiny crystals of chemicals which give off pulses of laser light when excited by electricity. Laser light is not like ordinary light, but consists of just one wavelength concentrated into a straight beam.

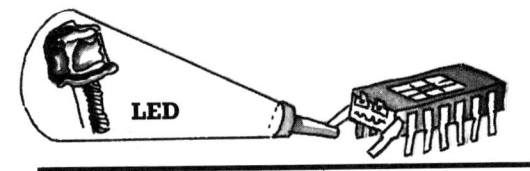

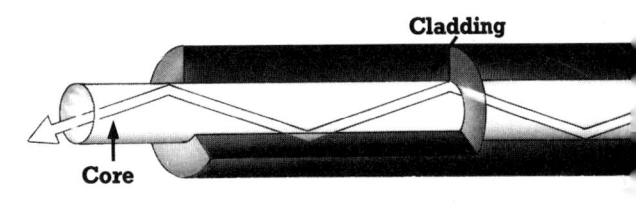

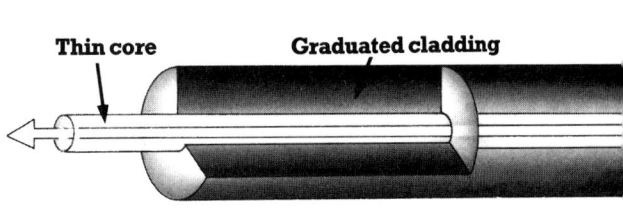

Transmitting signals

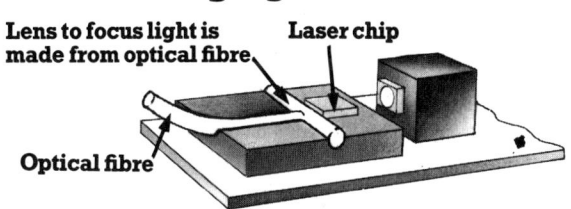

Signals transmitted by optical fibres can be analogue or digital. The message is turned into an electric current, which is used to excite the laser chip, or LED, into producing flashes of light. These light flashes have to be focused into the optical fibre by a lens which is also made from an optical fibre. The light travels along the fibre to the receiving end. Here there is a photodetector which converts the light back into an electric current. This electric current is then decoded back into its original form.

Messages in packets

With a digital transmission system, cables can carry individual messages chopped up into lots of little digital packets of about 10 bits, stacked with packets from other messages. Packets from phone calls, cable TV, computer data, viewdata and so on, can all travel together stacked in the same cable. The packets are sorted and put back together at the receiving end to form the original messages. Packets making up a single message even travel along different cables to reach the same destination at the same time. This allows the most efficient use of available cables. These techniques can be used with ordinary cables as well as optical fibres.

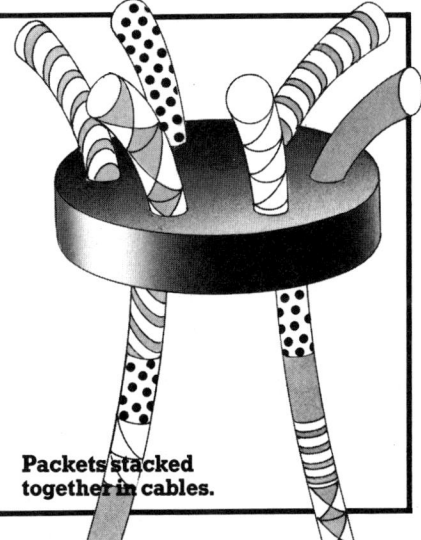

The revolution in factories

Office work has only recently been affected by microelectronics and computers, but other industries have been quicker to automate and use new technology. Most industries are concerned with making things, from aircraft to currant buns. Computers can operate machines and control manufacturing processes such as chemical production. Computers are also widely used to help in the initial design of products. Here are just some of the developments that have been taking place in industry.

Computer aided design (CAD)

Design is a big growth area for computers in industry. They are being used to help design things as diverse as cars and shoes. With the right sort of program a designer can make the computer simulate what will happen if a particular design is built. By changing aspects of the design, the designer can see what is likely to occur as a result. The computer saves the designer from actually building unsuitable designs, just to find out that they do not work. The computer can also show what will happen under different conditions – say to a bridge in various winds. Computers can also work out the most economical way of making something out of the materials available.

Computer monitors the temperature and controls pouring of molten metal in automated steel works.

Computer aided manufacture (CAM)

Machines that have to do the same thing over and over again can be operated automatically by a computer. The computer's program tells it how to control the machine and as software is easy to change this kind of control is very flexible. For example a lathe, used for turning and shaping things, can be programmed to move in various ways to make different products.

Computer control is also being applied to industrial processing, such as brewing, chemical manufacture, baking, oil refining and so on. Computers are very good at monitoring situations and responding to feedback. Heavy industries, such as mining and steel making, are using computers too.

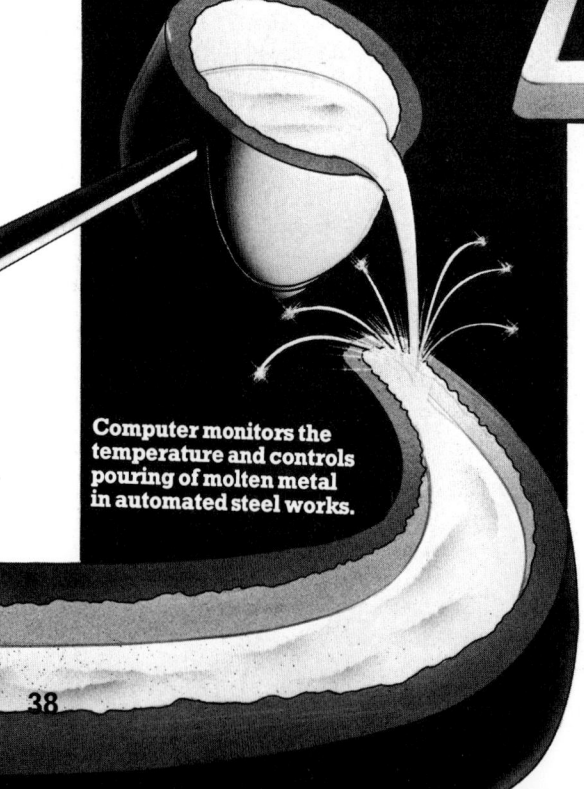

Robots

Robots are automatic machines which can be programmed to carry out lots of different jobs. Most of the robots used in factories are simply mechanical arms with a tool at the end, put to work on production lines. They cut, weld, rivet, paint, lift, pack and carry out many of the jobs necessary to make cars, washing machines, TVs and almost anything else. Robots are not intelligent, but simply move in response to instructions which take the form of a computer program. The computer runs the program and sends signals to the robot, making it move in the correct way to do what it is supposed to. Robots are very versatile and can perform lots of different jobs if given new software and tools. For example a paint spraying robot can be "re-trained" to weld.

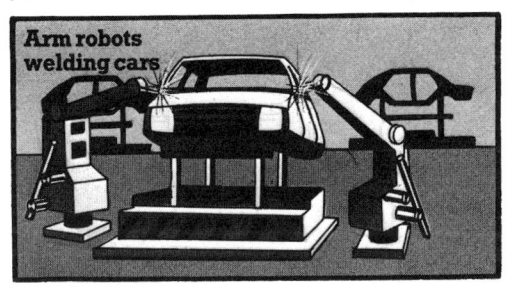

The latest robots are equipped with electronic sensors, such as video camera "eyes", microphone "ears", sonar or radar measuring and navigation devices and touch sensors. The robot uses these to send information back to its controlling computer. The computer is programmed to use this feedback to modify its instructions to the robot, in response to what is happening. A robot can be made to remove broken biscuits from a conveyor belt if it has a camera eye and its computer is programmed to recognize mishapen biscuits for instance.

Arm robots welding cars

Robots packing boxes

Rough design — **Computer works out cutting program.** — **Computer-controlled cutting robot.** — **Automatic sewing machine**

Future applications

Eventually the most advanced systems will link together CAD, CAM, robots and other automated machinery. A computer will be used to get the best possible design for a product and then put this information into the program which instructs the computer-controlled machines and robots that are making the finished product. The example above shows how a designer might design a pair of shoes, use the computer to work out the best cutting pattern for different sizes and then program the cutting and sewing robots with this information.

The people in charge of a factory would not actually have to be there. They could instruct and monitor the machines from home or an office, using computers linked by telecommunications to the factory. Sensors on the robots and video cameras in the factory could be used to send information back to the staff to show what was happening.

Video technology

Video is a way of electronically recording pictures and sounds on tape or disc. Television studios use video for recording programmes and an increasing number of feature films are being put on video so that you can buy or rent them to watch at home on your TV set. Video tape is good for making home movies, too, as it is cheaper and easier to use than ordinary film. Discs are the latest video development and you can see here how they differ from tape.

Cameras and recorders

Pictured on the right is a portable, home video camera. When used with a video cassette recorder it will make tapes of what you shoot, or you can plug it directly into your TV for instant display.

The light and sound from the scene you are shooting is turned into a stream of electronic signals by the camera. The recorder changes these signals into magnetic pulses and records them on a magnetic tape cassette in the machine.

This camera has a tiny TV screen as its viewfinder.

Video cassette player/recorder

Sound is recorded on the edge of the tape and pictures diagonally in the middle.

Video cassette player/recorders

A video cassette player turns the magnetic pulses recorded on the tape back into electronic signals. These are turned into pictures and sound again by your TV set, just as broadcast TV signals are. Most home video cassette machines record as well as play tapes. You can use them to tape ordinary TV programmes to watch later. This is known as off-air taping. The machine does not get the broadcast signals from your TV set, but has its own built-in TV tuner and receiver. So you can watch a programme on one channel, while your recorder tapes another at the same time.

Moving pictures

Moving pictures are recorded on video as still pictures, called frames, one at a time. They are played back very fast (25 frames a second in the UK and Europe, 30 frames a second in the USA and Japan) to give the effect of a moving image. The player can freeze a single frame to show a still picture. You can also play the video at different speeds for slow and fast motion and run it backwards.

Video discs

Video discs are similar in shape and size to audio LPs. At the moment you can only play pre-recorded video discs, not record them yourself, and you need a special video disc player to do so (just like with audio tapes and discs).

There are two different types of video disc. One is recorded and played using a stylus in a similar way to audio discs. The other uses a thin laser beam. Laser discs look like silvery mirrors and reflect light in rainbow colours. As they are played by a laser beam which does not actually touch the disc, they cannot be worn out. The reflective layer which holds the recording is covered by a thin coating of clear plastic which lets the laser beam through, but makes the disc so tough it will play perfectly even when covered in scratches and fingerprints. The other sort of disc is black and rainbow-shiny but must not be handled and is kept in a protective sleeve.

Interactive video discs

When you play a video tape, you have to watch it in sequence, waiting while the tape runs fast if you want to miss a bit. With a disc, you have "random access" to any part of it, which means you can tell the player which frame you want and it will play it instantly. You can control the order of the frames and the way in which they are played, and this is called "interactive" or "active play" video.

Every frame is numbered, like the pages of a book, and they can be grouped together into chapters. You can call up individual frames or chapters, or tell the player in what sequence to play them. Still frames made up of text and illustrations can be recorded on the disc with the ordinary video sections. The still frames can include things like multiple choice questions on the previous chapter. If you give the wrong answer, the player may automatically offer to show the relevant part of the video again. Some players contain microchips for control and to monitor your responses. Interactive video discs are useful for education and training, and even used in shops as an animated catalogue of goods.

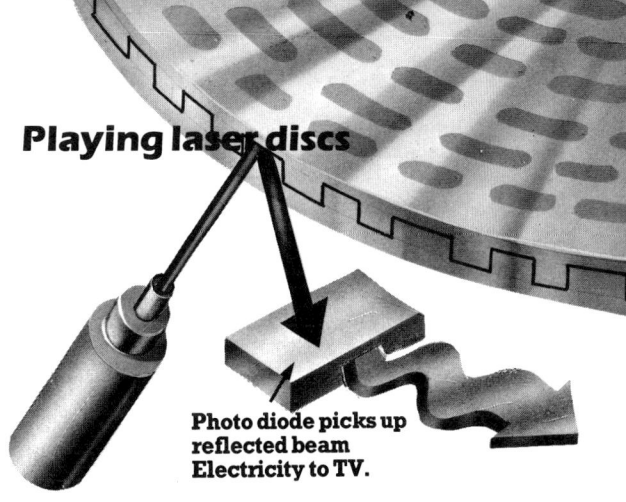

Playing laser discs

Photo diode picks up reflected beam Electricity to TV.

The picture and sound information is stored on the disc as a spiral of microscopic pits in a reflective layer, under the clear plastic coating. The laser beam in the player focuses on the reflective layer and is bounced back to a photo diode. The tiny pits change the reflection sent back to the photo diode, making it produce a varying current of electricity. This is turned by your TV back into the sound and pictures that were originally recorded. The information on laser discs is analogue, not digital as you might expect.

Computer control

Disc is played following instructions sent out by computer.

Disk drive plays computer program

Some video disc players can be controlled with a home computer. A program tells it which frames to show, when and how to play them, whether to change the speed, freeze or repeat a frame to alter the original video. With this sort of control, the information on a single video disc can be used in lots of different ways, simply by writing new software.

Microchips

Without microelectronics, and particularly the silicon chip, the information revolution would not be happening. Almost everything covered in this book works by microelectronics. Chips are so small and cheap to produce that they are making complex, versatile machines available to everyone.

Electronics

All electronic equipment – TVs, radios, phones, computers and so on – work because of tiny electric currents flowing round specially designed circuits. These circuits are formed from different kinds of components, such as transistors, diodes, capacitors and relays which control the flow of electricity through the circuit. The picture below compares the components you would need to make a simple radio circuit yourself, with a chip that does the same job.

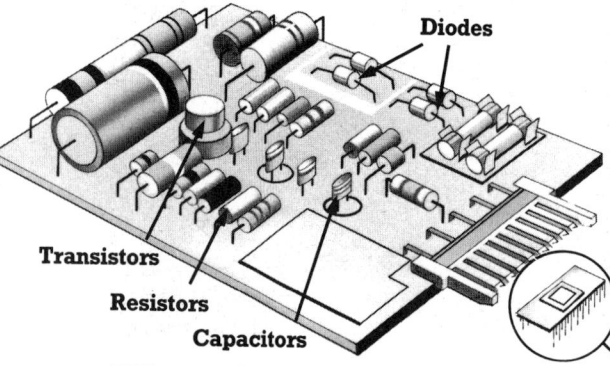

Diodes
Transistors
Resistors
Capacitors

What are chips?

This picture shows a close up of a "computer on a chip" of the kind used to make electronic machines "intelligent". All chips are made from wafer thin slices of chemicals called semi-conductors, the most commonly used is silicon. Semi-conductors conduct electricity – not as well as true conductors such as metals, but much better than non-conductors (called insulators) like wood.

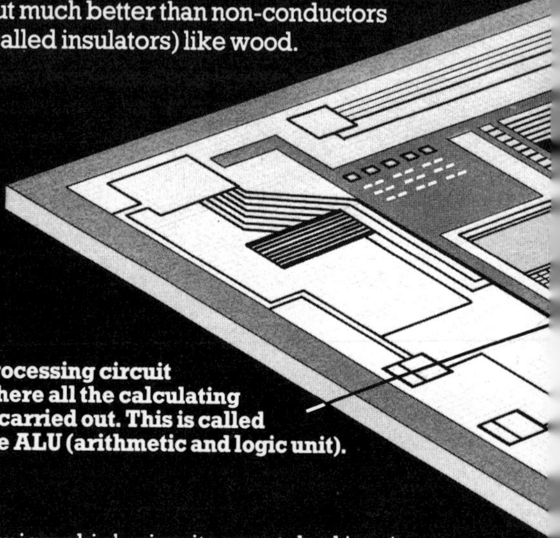

Processing circuit where all the calculating is carried out. This is called the ALU (arithmetic and logic unit).

A microchip's circuits are etched into its surface. The components and pathways for electricity to flow along are formed by adding tiny amounts of conductors and insulators which change the conducting ability of the semi-conducting surface.

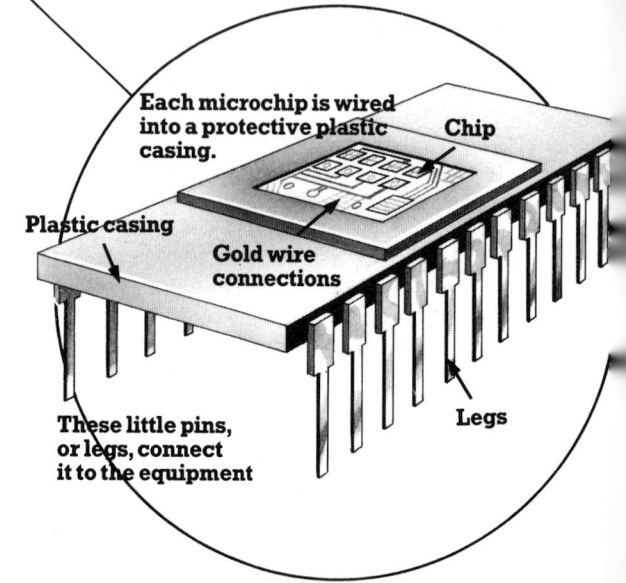

Microelectronics and chips

Microelectronics is electronics on a microscopic scale. Thousands of minute components and circuits can be crammed onto a tiny microchip, also known as an integrated circuit, only a few millimetres square. Their smallness gives microchips several advantages. Obviously they take up less space and so lots of them can be fitted inside a machine, giving increased processing power. They also work faster because the electricity has only a tiny journey to make flowing round a microscopically small circuit. Another great advantage is that chips are cheap to make as they are produced in vast quantities.

Each microchip is wired into a protective plastic casing.
Chip
Plastic casing
Gold wire connections
These little pins, or legs, connect it to the equipment
Legs

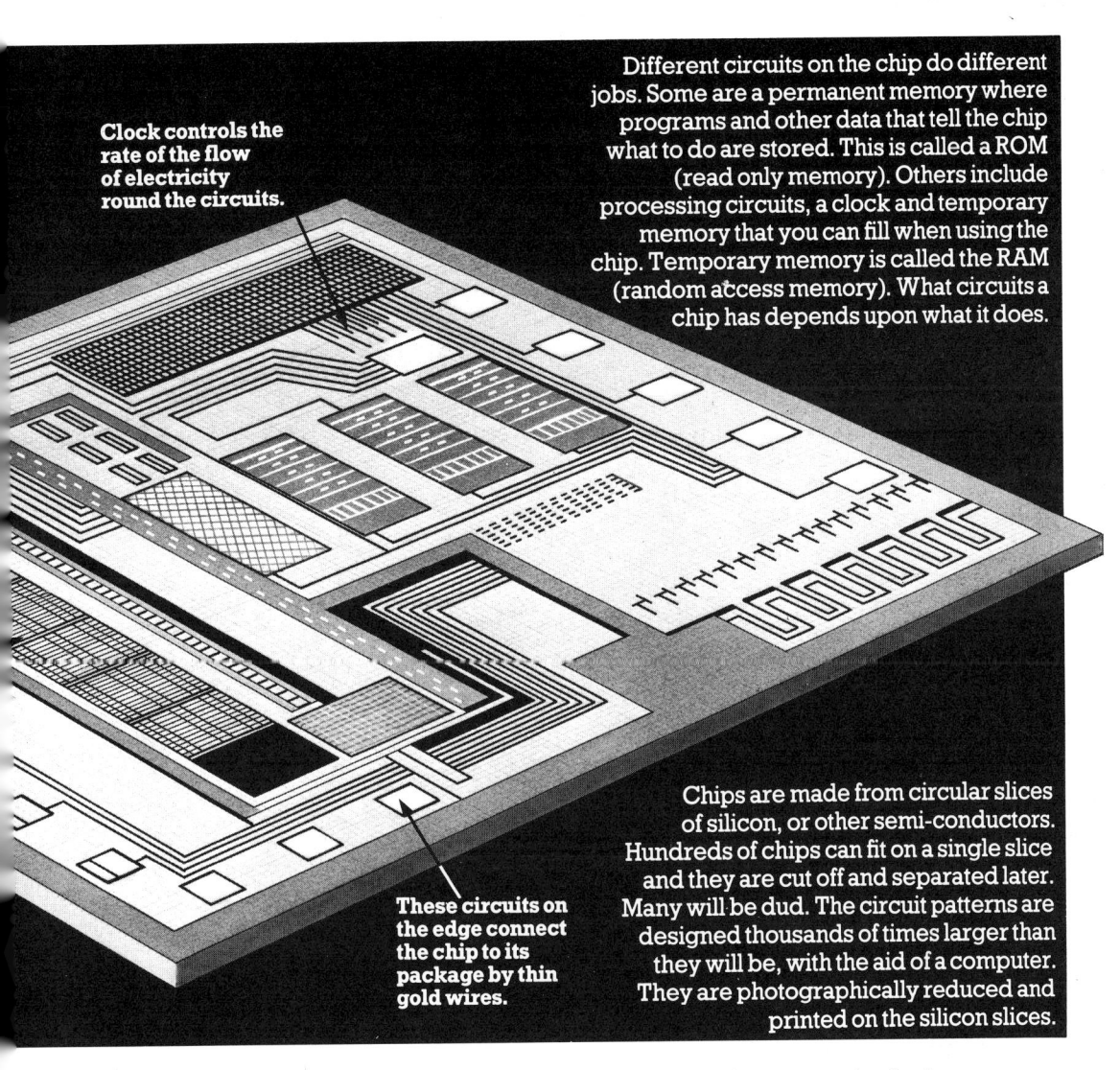

Clock controls the rate of the flow of electricity round the circuits.

Different circuits on the chip do different jobs. Some are a permanent memory where programs and other data that tell the chip what to do are stored. This is called a ROM (read only memory). Others include processing circuits, a clock and temporary memory that you can fill when using the chip. Temporary memory is called the RAM (random access memory). What circuits a chip has depends upon what it does.

These circuits on the edge connect the chip to its package by thin gold wires.

Chips are made from circular slices of silicon, or other semi-conductors. Hundreds of chips can fit on a single slice and they are cut off and separated later. Many will be dud. The circuit patterns are designed thousands of times larger than they will be, with the aid of a computer. They are photographically reduced and printed on the silicon slices.

Kinds of chips

There are many different kinds of chip, designed to do different jobs. A phone, for example, might have a modem chip to turn the incoming analogue signals into digital data, a memory chip to store phone numbers, control chips to carry out functions like automatic dialling and call routing, a character generating chip to work the VDU screen, a speech synthesizer chip and recording chips for messages, a laser chip in a fibre optic system and a microprocessor to organize and control them all.

Chips are programmed and given any special data they need to carry out their tasks when they are made. As they are specialized, or dedicated, in this way you could not take the chips out of a washing machine and use them in your home computer. However, the same design of chip can be programmed in many ways for different, but similar, uses.

Communicating with computers

In order to use the computerized new technology you have to be able to put in commands and information (known as input), get a response (known as output) and possibly store data for later use. There are lots of ways of communicating with computers and some are more obvious than others. A keyboard, for example, is more apparent than a pressure sensor that alerts a microprocessor if you do not put on your seat belt in a car. These pages look at some of the input, output and storage devices used with computers today.

Home computer

Alphanumeric keyboard

Keyboards

Typing at a keyboard is the most familiar way of inputting information. Home computers, terminals in banks and shops, videotex, phones and even digital watches all have some kind of keyboard. When you press a key this produces a coded electrical current that the computer recognizes as "b" or "B", "2" or a command such as "set the alarm". The kind of keyboard will depend upon the function of the machine. Many have letters and number plus special command keys.

Magnetic storage

Tapes, disks and stripes like those on bank cards are all ways of storing information magnetically. The digital data is sent to a recorder as pulses of electricity and these magnetize tiny particles of iron oxide on the surface of the tape, disk or stripe. "On" pulses make the particles face one way, "off" pulses make them face the other. The data is read by a magnetic sensor which turns the two magnetic fields back into electrical pulses. This is the most widespread way of storing computer data and it is erasable.

Disk

Tape in cassette

Reading

Computers can be taught to read but they have to memorize the shapes of all the characters (letters, numbers, symbols) for every different typeface they will come across. Computers read printing by scanning the page with a sensor. This produces on signals where ink is present and off signals where the page is blank and so the computer "sees" the characters as if they are 1s in a grid of 0s, like the picture above. Optical sensors work by reflecting light from the page and magnetic sensors read magnetic ink.

Pressure sensors

These can be used to "read" handwriting. The computer memorizes your signature if you sign your name several times, resting on a pressure sensitive pad. It turns the pressure and position of the pen into a digital number and can then compare these with your signature later, say on a cheque signed on another pressure sensor. Pressure sensors can also be used to tell if someone is sitting in a seat and to make a voice synthesizer chip speak to them, or to tell where someone is pointing on a touch sensitive screen.

Pressure sensitive pad tells the computer where the writing is.

44

Speech synthesis

Speech synthesizer chips have all the sounds that go to make up words stored in their memories. These sounds are known as phonemes. The chip produces them when letters are typed at a keyboard. Other chips have whole sentences digitally recorded in their memories and speak in response to certain input – the chip above is linked to a smoke detector, for example. Computerized telephones and exchanges use speech synthesis to pass on information to callers.

Hearing

Teaching a computer to understand speech is harder than getting it to talk. Although computers can be given electronic ears with simple microphones, it is difficult to program them to recognize complex sounds like speech, because people's voices are so variable. A computer can learn to recognize a few simple commands but it has to memorize every person's voice separately. An experimental dictation typewriter took 100 minutes to process and type a sentence that took just 30 seconds to say.

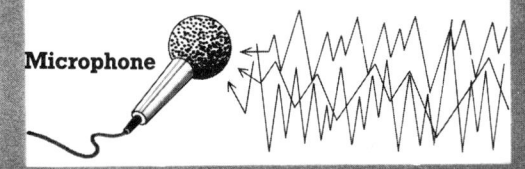

Optical storage

These systems can use the same reflective material as audio and video laser discs. Digital data is stored as pits and flats (no pits) in the reflective layer. When scanned by a laser the pits and flats reflect the beam differently, producing on/off electrical signals in a photo diode. A single laser disc can hold half a million pages of writing. Bar codes are another kind of optical storage system where the on/off signals are produced by a light reflected on black and white stripes.

Computer control

Computer control is used with all sorts of machines and processes – robots, model railways, steel-making, washing machines, digital watches, calculators and telephone exchanges are just a few examples. The controlling computer may be a whole machine that can be reprogrammed to do any kind of job and control any other machine, or just a few, permanently built-in microprocessors and other chips pre-programmed and dedicated to doing a single thing.

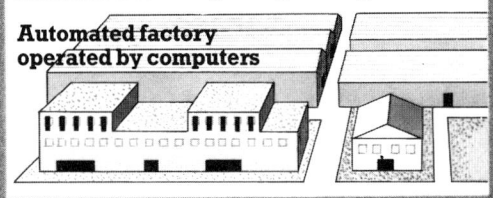

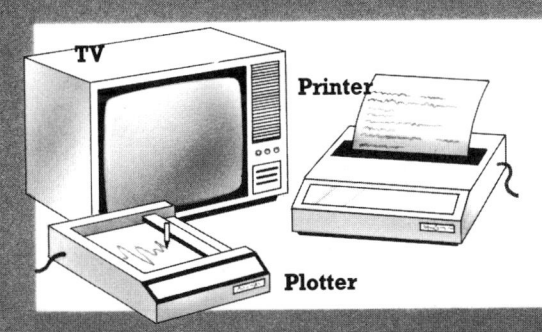

Automated factory operated by computers

Writing and pictures

The most usual kind of output is writing and pictures – known as text and graphics. This can be displayed on a screen or printed or drawn by computer-controlled electronic machines like printers and plotters. Screens and printers are used with all kinds of computers, like those in shops.

45

Information revolution words

Access: Getting data out of a computer or its database.

Acoustic coupler: A kind of modem (see below) where the handset of the phone fits into two cups. The acoustic coupler turns computer data into sounds and vice versa.

Analogue: This word actually means "similar to", but in computing it means "smoothly changing" – the opposite of digital.

Automation: Making machines carry out jobs without the constant help of people. Automatic machines are often controlled by computer or microchips.

Bar code: A pattern of black and white stripes that represents digital data.

BASIC: A computer language used for writing computer programs. It stands for Beginner's All-purpose Symbolic Instruction Code.

Bit: A binary digit either a 0 or a 1. In a computer bits are represented by on/off pulses of electricity.

Byte: A group of eight bits. Bytes are used to represent single pieces of information, such as a number, letter or symbol.

Cellular telephones: A radio telephone system where small areas, called cells, are each covered by a radio transmitter and form a network of overlapping cells.

Chip: See microchip, below.

Computer: An electronic calculating machine that can process information and follows instructions given to it in the form of a program.

Data: This is another word for information, used particularly to refer to the information that a computer deals with.

Database: An electronic store of information that can be used in a variety of ways by computers.

DBS (direct broadcast by satellite): TV broadcast via satellite, picked up by your own dish aerial.

Disk: A magnetic, or "floppy", disk stores data for use with a computer. They are played and recorded on a machine called a disk drive.

Digital: This word means dealing with numbers. Computers can only work with digital information where everything has been turned into binary digits.

Diode: An electronic component that allows electricity to flow one-way only.

Direct coupler: A modem that connects a computer directly to the phone line, by-passing the handset.

Electronic funds transfer (EFT): Taking money from one bank account and putting it in another electronically, using computers and telecommunications.

Frame: A videotex page (see below) or any single screen-sized picture, such as the frames of a film or video.

Gateway: The link of a computer database into the viewdata system, so that people can look at the information in it.

Input: Information that is put into a computer for processing.

Integrated circuit (IC): Another name for a microchip.

Keyword search: A way of getting information from a database by giving the computer a key word or phrase to look up.

Laser: Laser light is made up of just one wavelength in a concentrated, straight beam. The word stands for, Light Amplification by Stimulated Emission of Radiation.

LCD (liquid crystal display): A kind of screen used to display information.

LED (light emitting diode): A diode (see above) which produces light in response to electricity.

Machine code: A computer language made up of the bits and bytes that a computer can actually understand.

Microchip: A tiny, electronic device containing many components and circuits etched onto the surface of a semi-conducting material like silicon.

Microwave: A kind of short radio wave used for telecommunications.

Modem: A device that turns computer data into a signal which can travel over the phone, and vice versa. The word is short for modulator/demodulator.

On-line: When a terminal, phone or other equipment is connected directly to a computer, it is said to be on-line.

Optical fibre: A very thin strand of glass or plastic that can carry light. Used in telecommunications.

Output: Information that comes out of a computer.

Packet switching: Sending messages as small, digital packets that can travel through a telecommunications system independently of each other. They are reassembled at the receiving end.

Page: A videotex term used to describe a screen-sized display of information. Also known as a frame.

Pixel: Short for picture cell. Screens are divided up into a grid of pixels and images are made by picture generating chips which light up the pixels in response to signals from a computer.

Program: A sequence of instructions which will make a computer carry out a job. They are written in computer languages such as BASIC and machine code.

Random access: When using a tape to store information you have to run it backwards and forwards to get to the parts you want. A random access system allows you to jump instantly from one part to another without waiting. Random access can be provided by memory circuits on a chip, by magnetic disks and laser discs.

Software: Another name for computer programs. The actual computer, which runs the software, is referred to as hardware.

Speech synthesis: Electronically generated speech which is made up from sounds that have been digitally recorded, often on chips.

Terminal: A computer keyboard, or other input device, that does not have its own computing power but is linked to a distant computer and database.

Telesoftware; Computer programs which are loaded straight into your computer by videotex. In Britain telesoftware is provided as viewdata on *Prestel* by *Micronet*, and as teletext by the BBC's *Ceefax*. *Comp-U-Serve* supplies viewdata telesoftware in North America.

Teletext: Broadcast information from distant computers which can be displayed on your TV screen. The two teletext services in Britain are *Ceefax*, run by the BBC, and *Oracle*, run by the ITV. In North America various teletext services are being offered on a trial basis, such as *keyfax, IRIS* and *Extravision*.

Videotex: Information from distant computers displayed on a TV screen. It can reach you as TV broadcasts (known as teletext) and by phone or cable TV (known as viewdata). As these are very new developments these terms may be used differently by other books and magazines. Videotex is often used to mean viewdata, for example.

Viewdata: A two-way communications system where you can get information from distant computers and respond to it. Viewdata works by phone, or by interactive cable TV. In Britain viewdata is called *Prestel*, in Canada it is called *Telidon*. North America has *Comp-U-Serve* and *The Source* which provide home computer owners with access to databases and services such as teleshopping and banking and electronic mail.

Voice message: A digitally recorded message that accompanies text and graphics on screen, or is played to pass on information automatically.

Word processor: A computer used for writing, editing, storing and manipulating typed text.

Work station: An electronic "desk" made up of a computer, phone and links to a central computer, database, other work stations and equipment like printers.

Index

acoustic coupler, 19, 25
analogue, 8, 32, 33, 41
audio tapes and discs, 41

bank, 3, 4, 12, 13, 21, 32
bar code, 9, 10, 11, 14, 45
BASIC, 27
binary, 8
bit, 8, 15, 33, 37
byte, 8

cable, 3, 4
   TV, 4, 14, 13, 15, 16-21
CAD (computer aided design), 38, 39
calculator, 6, 7, 14
CAM (computer aided manufacture), 38, 39
camera, 7
car, 7, 44
cash dispenser, 13
cassette, 6, 11, 24
cellular phones, 31
chips, 3, 6, 7, 13, 15, 17, 19, 23, 28, 30, 40, 41, 42, 43
closed user group, 20
cursor, 28

database, 4, 18, 20, 24, 30, 34
DBS, 14, 15, 34, 35
debit card, 12, 13
digital, 8, 9, 33, 41
direct coupler, 19
dish aerial, 9, 14, 34, 35
disk, 9, 20, 25, 26, 28

editing, 28
electromagnetic spectrum, 36
electronic funds transfer (EFT), 12, 13
electronic mail, 4, 6, 18, 26
electronic office, 26, 27, 32

facsimile machine, 4, 32
factories, 5, 38, 39

feedback, 39
Financial Times, 34
footprint, 34, 35
frames, 17, 40, 41

gateway, 21
geosynchronous orbit, 34, 35

high definition (HD) TV, 15

information provider, 20
information technology, 3, 4
infra-red, 22, 36
insulators, 42
integrated circuit, 42

keyboard, 18, 28, 44
keypad, 22

laser, 3, 4, 8, 11, 37, 41, 45
LCD, 14
LED, 11, 37

machine code, 27
magnetic stripe, 12
memory card, 13
memory chip, 3, 10
microchip, 3, 6, 7, 13, 15, 17, 19, 23, 28, 30, 40, 41, 42, 43
microelectronics, 3, 4, 7, 27, 30, 38
microphone, 33, 39, 45
microwave, 31, 34, 35, 36
Microwriter, 29
modem, 6, 18, 19, 25, 26, 29

network, 26

optical fibres, 3, 4, 8, 33, 36, 37
optical storage, 45

packets, 37
photodetector, 10, 37
PIN (personal identity number), 12, 13

pits, 9, 45
pixels, 17, 18
program, 3, 7, 9, 10, 21, 24, 25, 28, 29, 41

radio, 7
RAM (random access memory), 43
robot, 5, 7, 34, 38, 39, 45
ROM (read only memory), 43

satellite, 6, 8, 9, 26, 31, 34, 35
   TV, 5, 14
semi-conductor, 42, 43
sensors, 29, 44
shopping, 3, 10, 11, 32
silicon, 42
software, 5, 18, 19, 24, 25, 28, 29, 41
space travel, 7
speech synthesis, 7, 31, 33, 44, 45
spelling program, 29

telebanking, 3, 4, 5, 12, 13
telecommunications, 8, 30-33, 34
telephone, 6, 9, 30-33
teleshopping, 4, 32
telesoftware, 20, 24, 25
teletext, 16, 22, 23
television, 14, 15, 17, 18, 23, 40, 41
terminal, 10, 11, 12, 13
thesaurus program, 29
transaction telephone, 13

USA Today, 34

video, 5, 14, 29, 40, 41
   disc, 5, 7, 14, 21, 40, 41
videotex, 4, 6, 16-27
viewdata, 13, 14, 16-21, 24, 25, 30
viewphones, 21
visual display unit (VDU), 26, 28
voice messages, 27, 30

word processing, 27, 28, 29
work station, 26, 27, 34

Books to read

If you want to find out more about some of the things mentioned in this book, such as TV and video, computers and programming, BASIC, chips and electronics, here are some useful books to read. They are all published by Usborne Publishing.

TV & Video C. Griffin-Beale

Computers B. Reffin Smith

Understanding the Micro
J. Tatchell & B. Bennett

Introduction to Computer Programming
B. Reffin Smith

Computer Jargon L. Watts & C. Stockley

Better BASIC B. Reffin Smith & L. Watts

Inside the Chip H. Davies & M. Wharton

Fun With Electronics J. G. McPherson

The name Usborne and the device are Trade Marks of Usborne Publishing Ltd.